If you are raising child. ... . you haven't meditated before, *Mindful Parenting in a Messy World* is for you. Michelle knows her subject from the inside out and delivers the wisdom of her experience with humor and honesty. This deeply helpful book for parents is wonderful to read.

Sharon Salzberg, author of *Real Happiness* and *Real Love*

I think it's safe to assume many of us struggle with how to balance being a lovingly engaged parent while also trying to maintain a household, honor our work and social commitments, and maintain our sanity. That may explain why I breathed easier every time I opened *Mindful Parenting in a Messy World.* Nourished by Michelle Gale's gentle wisdom, relatable anecdotes, and practical strategies, I felt empowered to enrich my family's experience of everyday life. *Mindful Parenting in a Messy World* reveals how mindfulness can ground parents moment-to-moment, even amidst chaos, and find peace together and within.

Rachel Macy Stafford, New York Times bestselling author of *Hands Free Mama, Hands Free Life,* and *Only Love Today*

"I love Michelle. Her book is a helpful guide, with a lot of experience packed into it, for anyone who wants to learn how to be a better parent."

Byron Katie

This is likely the most honest description of what genuine mindfulness means for our everyday lives that you will ever read. This is the story of a mother who lays out her struggles as an individual, a wife, and a parent in a manner that causes us to laugh and cry with her—and simultaneously admire her—as she tells of her messy journey and shows us what it really means to be mindful. There's no perfectionism here, no "getting there," and certainly no "arriving," just invaluable insight and wisdom concerning how an ordinary person can begin living in an extraordinary manner.

Dr Shefali Tsabary, author of the Oprah-acclaimed The Conscious Parent, Out of Control, and The Awakened Family

Michelle Gale's engaging journey has a profoundly liberating message for us all: life is messy, relax and embrace it, you don't have to be perfect. She delivers practical advice through funny and brutally honest stories, showing the way to each of us who longs to be more present with our children and with ourselves.

James Gimian, Founder of Mindful Magazine

I can think of no one better to guide us through the art of mindful parenting than Michelle Gale. As she says in her exquisite book, this is not about being a "good parent." It is about waking up through the act of parenting.

Soren Gordhamer, Founder of Wisdom 2.0

Mindful Parenting in a Messy World is an invitation and a road-map. Michelle Gale shows us how to use daily life, parenting, and family, as the curriculum for becoming present, aware, and compassionate. She wisely and gently helps us remember to stay awake during difficult times in parenting and in life, so that we can come home to ourselves.

Jason and Cecilia Hilkey, founders of Happily Family

Michelle Gale shares through her own path of learning, how the difficulties of life and parenting can also be the greatest opportunity for inner growth.

Ruchika Sikri, Manager of Sustainable Performance and Well-being at Google

Mindful Parenting in a Messy World is a parents' guidebook to living with greater presence and awareness in our modern times. It's totally relatable, non-judgmental, and incredibly insightful.

Lin-Hua Wu, VP of Communications at Dropbox

MINDFUL PARENTING IN A MESSY WORLD

LIVING WITH PRESENCE AND PARENTING WITH PURPOSE

MICHELLE GALE

MOtivational PRESS®

LEADERS IN GLOBAL PUBLISHING

Published by Motivational Press, Inc.
1777 Aurora Road
Melbourne, Florida, 32935
www.MotivationalPress.com

Manufactured in the United States of America.

ISBN:

CONTENTS

PRAISE FOR MINDFUL PARENTING IN A MESSY WORLD I

INTRODUCTION 1
Mindfulness and Messiness

CHAPTER 1 6
Breathing Space

CHAPTER 2 15
The Path of Growth Lies in Awareness

CHAPTER 3 23
The Family as Catalyst for Personal Development

CHAPTER 4 31
Awareness Enters the Picture

CHAPTER 5 36
Finding Meditation

CHAPTER 6 48
Searching for our True Self

CHAPTER 7 56
How Having a Family of My Own Grew Me Up

CHAPTER 8 62
The Challenge of the Teen Years

CHAPTER 9 70
Pain as a Portal to Consciousness

CHAPTER 10 75
Life Plays Its Hand

CHAPTER 11 79
Don't Avoid the Pain

CHAPTER 12 85
Returning to Work after Baby

CHAPTER 13 98
Practicing Mindfulness as a Family

CHAPTER 14 107
The Punishment Trap

CHAPTER 15 114
When I "Lose It"

CHAPTER 16 121
Growing Mindfulness

CHAPTER 17 125
Gifting Children with Our Presence

CHAPTER 18 133
Who Am I and What Do I Need?

CHAPTER 19 143
Just Say No

CHAPTER 20 149
My Messy Spirituality

ACKNOWLEDGEMENTS 154

ABOUT THE ILLUSTRATORS 156

"*Parenting is one of the most challenging, demanding, and stressful jobs on the planet. It is also one of the most important, for how it is done influences in great measure the heart and soul of consciousness of the next generation, their experience of meaning and connection, their repertoire of life skills, and their deepest feelings about themselves and their possible place in a rapidly changing world.*"

-Jon and Myla Kabat-Zinn
Everyday Blessings: The Inner Work
of Mindful Parenting

For Tyler and Brody. Your inner wisdom inspires me every day. Being your mom is the greatest privilege of my life.

INTRODUCTION

MINDFULNESS AND MESSINESS

"Mindfulness is simply being aware of what is happening right now without wishing it were different; enjoying the pleasant without holding on when it changes (which it will); being with the unpleasant without fearing it will always be this way (which it won't)."

– James Baraz, Author of Awakening Joy for Kids

MINDFULNESS

Before I launch into my stories, learnings, and suggestions, I want to clear up the definition of mindfulness and meditation from my perspective so we are all on the same page. Mindfulness in its most simple definition is a map for understanding the human experience. The core of the practice has us practicing and resting in presence, allowing us to know what is being known. It is a compassionate non-judgmental awareness of our inner and outer moment to moment experience. No part of our human understanding is left out of the practice. And ultimately, there is no one definition of mindfulness that will ever encompass everything. I suggest you hold any definition you read lightly, but learn what you can from each one. For the use of this book, I'll use the word meditation to refer to formal practice (like when we practice sitting or walking meditation) and the word mindfulness to refer to any way we direct our attention within ourselves or to the outside world.

I also want to mention that we can learn to be mindful in some zillion different ways. Practices like qigong, tai chi, yoga, journaling, painting, chanting, or so many other activities can support us on this path. Whatever works for you is the way to go. I will say that studying my mind with intention during formal meditation while also practicing presence while cultivating compassion and curiosity in my day to day life has been my lifeline to managing my anxiety, cultivating joy, and living with purpose.

I think it's just as important to talk about what mindfulness IS NOT because the word is starting to be overused in popular culture. Being mindful does not mean that you are calm all the time. You can just as easily be aware of your anxiety, anger, or fear, as you can be all Zen and relaxed. Don't get me wrong, I love it when practicing meditation or mindfulness brings me to a state of calm, but I don't at all expect that to be the case, nor should we expect constant calm and bliss while weaving in and out of family life. Are you with me?

> Being mindful does not mean that you are calm all the time. You can just as easily be aware of your anxiety, anger, or fear, as you can be all Zen and relaxed

The goal of meditation is not to stop thoughts. Thinking is part of being human and we should not beat ourselves up or call ourselves bad meditators because we can't stop thinking. In fact, when we sit in meditation and notice our mind has wandered... this is exactly why we practice. This means we are doing it right! In this moment of noticing our mind wander we learn that we have a choice. We can continue letting our mind do its thing or we can come back to focusing on the breath or another point of concentration. We practice so that in our day-to-day lives we have more choice as to where we put our attention, and how we show up in the world at any given moment. For me, one of my favorite outcomes of practice is to not take my stressful thoughts so seriously. I certainly still have them; they just don't run the show. So, when I'm thinking to myself, good lord I'm a terrible parent, why did I say that? I shouldn't have raised my voice or made that assumption or been so impatient. I have learned to take a breath, notice those thoughts and decide not to buy into them so heavily. In making this shift I'm kinder to myself and to others through the radical act of self-discovery.

Like anything else worth learning, mindfulness is a practice. Something we choose to spend concentrated effort on until it becomes our new normal. And make no mistake about it...living a mindful life is a blessing like no other. As we awaken to who we are we can live more fully and show up more authentically in every aspect of our lives. I have found in my own life that making this commitment to myself has not only supported me, but also my family, in ways I could never have imagined.

EMBRACING MESSINESS

So, what is all this talk about embracing messiness anyway? Holy cow, you guys, this is the best part of all! If there is one thing we can count on it is that things will change and our lives will go sideways when we least expect it. Sometimes it's just something mundane like the grocery store is out of the peanut butter our kids like (how rude) and other times "you know what" really hits the fan and someone in our family gets injured. As we practice mindfulness we learn to meet each moment with a sort of equanimity, not taking it all so personally. The mess of life will present itself over and over again. We can count on it. What if, instead of pushing away the icky parts and only welcoming the pleasant experiences we learned to embrace all of them? Jon Kabat-Zinn, who happens to be one of my favorite teachers, wrote a book over twenty-five years ago called "Full Catastrophe Living: Using the Wisdom of Your Body and Mind to Face Stress, Pain, and Illness". When I saw the title I nearly dropped to my knees. The first time I read this book I was single and not even thinking about a family. Reading it again so many years later after having two children, the message once again soothed my soul but for such different reasons.

It was clear to me that so much of my suffering as a parent came from the stress and anxiety of worrying that I might be screwing up my kids, and that I'm not a good parent. I was also a professional at wanting things to be different when they didn't go my way. What I've learned over the years is that it is precisely when things don't go my way that I have the most lessons to learn. This is the gift the mess gives me. Now, I would be lying if I didn't say that I certainly prefer when it's humming along smoothly in

> What I've learned over the years is that it is precisely when things don't go my way that I have the most lessons to learn. This is the gift the mess gives me.

all the right directions. I mean…duh. But over time, instead of cringing when life started to go sideways, I began to get curious and interested, in what life lesson may be awaiting me. This is not a path for the faint of heart. The mess of our lives can seriously suck. However, as it turns out, embracing reality is a much more peaceful way to live. May these stories and learnings serve you on your path to mindful living within the messiness of your life.

At the end of each chapter you will find a reflection, resource, or practice to support your path. You might find it helpful to journal as your read through each chapter, or utilize the practices and resources as you go along.

CHAPTER 1

BREATHING SPACE

Our parents, our children, our spouses, and our friends will continue to press every button we have, until we realize what it is that we don't want to know about ourselves, yet. They will point us to our freedom every time.

Byron Katie

YELLING AT MY CHILDREN makes me feel like the worst mom on the planet. Energy builds. I snap, raise my voice, and immediately I feel ashamed. Our connection to each other is lost and I pine to find my way back to myself and to them.

It became clear to me many years ago that whenever I would be getting upset and about to "blow", my body would be giving me all kinds of signs. You might see me pacing, cleaning up frantically, or tightening my jaw. Anyone who lived with me could see the frustration and rage building—anyone, that is, except myself.

That's why I enlisted my little guy's help.

At the tender age of four, Tyler had a far greater ability to see when mommy was about to lose her cool. The funny thing is, this was a time in my life when I was working with a somatic teacher to consciously learn what my body was trying to tell me about my internal state. I was practicing regularly, yet it took my sweet four-year-old to help me interrupt the pattern that caused me to yell and bring me to my knees with the dreaded mommy guilt.

Oh, mommy guilt. It's brutal.

I desperately wanted to end my tendency to react so strongly to the stressors in my life. Now, don't get me wrong. I wasn't yelling every moment of every day, but it certainly happened more than I personally felt comfortable with. I was ready for change.

I had asked Tyler if he would let me know whenever he noticed me becoming upset, suggesting he tell me I needed to stop and take a breath. We had made an agreement that whenever he uttered the words "Breathe, Momma" I would immediately stop. There would be no overriding what he was asking, no matter how powerfully the rising tide of emotion (and insanity) rose within me.

Hearing his little voice remind me to "Breathe, Momma" was precisely what I needed to hear. Dealing with the pressures of a career, while trying to be a sane parent and loving wife, I frequently found myself feeling frazzled and his little voice helped every time.

This simple practice of getting Tyler to help me check in with myself became a powerful tool for change. By stopping me in my tracks *before* I raised my voice, Tyler enabled me to begin to notice what was happening inside me that triggered my outbursts. I found myself floored early on in our little experiment as to how many times he noticed me getting agitated long before I caught on to it. To this day, many years later, Tyler will call me out on the rug if I need to stop and take a breath. He helped me begin to learn the power of awareness.

PUTTING MYSELF ON THE LINE

I'm not going to tell you that it was easy for me to enlist a child to change a pattern of behavior I didn't like about myself. To be honest, it felt a little silly at first. I will say that seeking Tyler's input turned out to be one of the most empowering things I've ever done.

And not just for myself, but for my son, his younger brother, and my husband. Becoming vulnerable in this way, admitting I had a huge flaw in my character, put our entire family in a growth mindset, helping us know for certain that we could work through our struggles together. I slowly became a lot more aligned with who I wanted to be, and deeper connection was growing within our family.

It's no walk in the park to be vulnerable. Who wants to feel like they are seriously flawed? That even my kids—*especially* my kids—see this about me? Brene Brown who is a brilliant researcher and storyteller tells us that vulnerability is the birthplace of love, belonging, joy, courage, empathy, and creativity. It is the source of hope, accountability, and authenticity. If we want greater clarity in our purpose, or deeper and more meaningful spiritual lives, vulnerability is the path. Hey, I'm not going to argue with Brene.

So, what did I do with the feeling of shame after yelling at these precious little people?

Instead of feeling forever horrible about needing to apologize over and over again, I took the step of *accepting* myself that day as someone who yelled *sometimes*. In this acceptance of reality, real change began.

This was a seriously scary leap for a woman who had followed the prescriptions of many a self-help bible in her struggle to change herself. I finally accepted that many of the books I'd looked to for answers would have been better named "shelf-help" books because I had often read them, put them back on the shelf...and gone right on doing the same old, same old.

Newsflash. Change is more challenging when we are down on who we are. Self-loathing breeds despair, not hope—and that's a recipe for a worsening situation, not transformation.

That's why all the books, all the talks, all the online courses didn't help...until I was willing to look square in the mirror and accept—no, *embrace!*—the person looking back. Welcome to reality and all the messiness that comes with it!

It was in total acceptance of myself exactly as I was—warts and all, that I began to find peace. From this place of surrender, real change began.

If I spent too much time feeling guilty, wallowing in denial, or deflecting my inner anger onto those around me, then frustration, a sense of hopelessness, and anger surfaced. Not the best way to cultivate a happy family. I've learned through studying non-violent communication that each time I'm struggling in life, one of my most basic human needs is not being met, and along with it some really big feelings appear.

It's really no different from when my youngest acts up or my teen acts out. In every case, some need isn't being met. Maybe I'm not hearing what's truly important to them, or perhaps I'm just not listening. What if their best friend is mad at them and they are experiencing loneliness or abandonment that day? Struggling with these needs and feelings comes out in rotten behavior. But it's never the behavior that's the issue, always the feeling behind it—the unmet need. As I learned to become aware of these feelings and needs, healing began. It sounds counterintuitive, but surrendering to these big feelings and needs while accepting them just as they are in that moment was my key to shifting everything.

For me, acceptance meant that whenever I yelled, I did my best to pause and take a breath as soon as possible while also getting a grip on *my tendency to feel awful about myself.*

I practiced not thinking of myself as a "bad mother." I accepted that my explosive emotions were often just trapped energy, the leftovers of ways I had learned to protect myself as a child. My behavior had nothing to do with being bad, and everything to do with patterns of self-defense established long ago at a time when they were absolutely necessary.

Having said this, I don't wish to imply that I let myself off the hook when my energy manifested itself in bad behavior. Accepting myself, including my crummy behavior, meant that these things were no longer moral issues. They were simply matters of practicality, involving nothing more than learning to use the energy more productively now that I'm no longer a child. It's a learning we all have to go through, and practicing mindfulness and meditation can really support this process. A good therapist works wonders too! I've been blessed to have a few of those over the years.

Instead of being down on myself, I began to see myself as a work in progress. I began to find that yummy inner peace that can seem so elusive.

TREASURE YOUR ICKY PARTS

This may seem crazy, but when I put myself on the line by owning my inability to control my periodic outbursts, it didn't generate scorn or disrespect from my family. On the contrary, they appreciated my willingness to take myself on.

You can't help but admire someone who faces up to himself or herself. It can be scary looking in that mirror!

It took courage and daring to embrace my icky parts. In the process of doing so, the awesome side effect was that my children learned to do the same. It's still a work in progress of course, but they have learned to accept that *their* seemingly icky parts are okay too. I believe for a child to grow up in a household where everyone is willing to embrace these baffling parts of themselves is an incredible gift.

Coming out of hiding and becoming more vulnerable enabled me to drop my defensiveness. I no longer needed to protect an image of myself as "the perfect parent," who's supposed to have it together. The words "perfection" and "parenting" honestly shouldn't even be permitted in the same sentence. Can we all just agree that it's perfectly fine to be a "good enough" parent?

I've heard it said that the greatest gift we can give our children is in getting ourselves together. There's certainly a truth in this. What I came to realize is that the way we do this is to first give ourselves permission to be okay with not having it together in the first place.

I can now give myself a break and understand that the magic is in

> The words "perfection" and "parenting" honestly shouldn't even be permitted in the same sentence. Can we all just agree that it's perfectly fine to be a "good enough" parent.

honestly and openly recovering from my bad behavior, neither pretending it doesn't exist nor beating myself up because of it. Coming clean about my flaws fostered a sense that we are all in this struggle to grow and change *together*. We're here to help each other by mirroring the ways in which we each have yet to grow up. Over time, my husband and I came to see that we had way more growing up to do than our boys, and they were the greatest teachers we could ask for.

ALL IN THE FAMILY

At any given time, most families will identify one member of the family as "the problem". More often than not, it's one of the children who is identified as having "the problem". From what I've seen in my own family, it is true that at any one time, one person is struggling more than the others. The focus then shines on that individual, who is seen as needing to be "fixed".

But what if that person's problem is everyone else's opportunity?

In my family, when one of our children is struggling, my husband and I look to ourselves first, seeking to understand why we are being triggered by this particular child's behavior.

I can't tell you how many times one of my boys was upset because they didn't have a friend to play with and I was just irate. Investigating myself, I realized that because I had been an only child I spent a lot of time alone, entertaining myself. How dare they not be able to entertain themselves the way I did! In having this realization, I was able to allow them their sadness in desiring play with a buddy without becoming furious about it. I mean, how many times can our kids hear us ask them to be grateful for what they have rather than what they don't have? Yes, it's all true…but perhaps we could hop off our high horse, take a peek at the situation without our clichés and meet them where they are.

I wouldn't want to underestimate how many times just looking deeply at ourselves ends the problem with our children. We make a small change and the child magically shifts.

After we investigate our inner world a bit we may actually be able to come up with a way to help them through their difficult patch. Can we help them? Is this something they need to figure out on their own with us acting as a net if they fall? Do they need outside support? Is this just a phase that we can let roll?

Kids are just being kids, doing what kids do, learning and growing, trying to find their way in the world. Let's do our best to normalize what's normal behavior while doing our own work to understand our triggers. And sometimes all that's required is for us to let them know we see them and are with them in their struggle. Compassion breeds connection every time.

Exercise

Taking intentional breaths throughout the day feels like a parenting superpower to me. Focusing on the breath can be a beautiful centering practice, but you have to build the muscle of this center in the same way that you have to build your muscles at the gym. Repetition is the key. Remember to focus on the inhale, as well as the exhale. Remind yourself to take these breaths by adding them to your calendar, write yourself reminder notes, or set an alarm on your phone—whatever it takes. Those few moments of stillness, during which I observe whatever I may have been thinking or feeling that triggered a reaction, enables me to put things in perspective, become better acquainted with myself, and get back on an even keel. As the Delphic Oracle says, "Know thyself." I couldn't agree more. Our breath is a pathway into who we truly are and supports who we are becoming. My friend Annmarie Chereso suggested the app "Mind Jogger" to help remind me when I'm working on a new behavior. It's a brilliant little tool.

> Our breath is a pathway into who we truly are and supports who we are becoming

CHAPTER 2

THE PATH OF GROWTH LIES IN AWARENESS

"There is only one moment in time when it is essential to awaken. That moment is now."

- Buddha

IMAGINE I'M NOT ALONE in having moments when I've said or acted in a destructive manner. Following this, as I come to my senses, I say something like, "Oh, my God, what have I done? What did I say?"

No matter how many times I do it, I'm actually shocked to see the damage I've done. I'm horrified at the unkind words I spoke, the stomping away, the pouty face I won't let go. It's painfully evident in these moments that I don't have much awareness.

In fact, we talk about someone "not being in his or her right mind." We also refer to people as "beside themselves" with anger. Or we say they "lost it." These, and similar expressions, suggest that we are acting from a lack of awareness. As I become defensive my sanity is eclipsed by the tidal wave of emotion that arises within me, I'm simply not very conscious of what I'm saying or doing. And by the way, I don't need to be angry in order to lose my awareness, I can do it simply by zoning out on my cell phone, being lost in thought as my child is speaking to me, or eating a meal and never tasting it.

The fact is, the path to growth isn't as elusive as it may seem. For me, it involves becoming *aware*. It also involves committing to practicing awareness, which is easier said than done, but so worth our effort.

When I speak of "awareness," I'm referring to noticing what's going on in and around me as my day unfolds. It's a matter of being tuned into what's happening, rather than painfully oblivious in the way so many of us are. It's not just me, right? Have you ever gotten in your car and driven somewhere having no memory of getting there? Yep, me too.

Practicing awareness allows me the opportunity to be deeply connected to my children and myself. I'm remembering when my boys were infants and I spent my days attuning to their every movement, every need. I looked into their eyes not thinking of anywhere else to go. I fed them and watched their little mouths receive the food, not being distracted by anything else. During these early months, a certain kind of peace fell over me that I had never experienced before. Stillness and presence were working their magic.

So, to cultivate more awareness, I started observing myself with curiosity, especially in response to the people around me and the many situations in which I found myself from day-to-day. This would all be much easier if we lived in complete isolation, but the reality is that being in relationship to others is sticky and messy. The good news is that other people give us plenty of chances to practice!

I slowly began to notice how thoughts come and go, emotions rise and fall, and which sensations are most alive within my body. For instance, one day I got into an argument with one of my children about not cleaning up their mess. In this moment, clearly not in the mood for my anger, they went into their room and slammed the door. I really wanted to jump up and go after them, yelling, "How dare you slam the door on me?" But as I just sat with this surge of emotions, sensations, and sadistic thoughts for a few moments, they subsided. Honestly, they did. Then I suddenly realize that I've slammed doors too. When I finally re-engaged with them again I was able to connect, rather than just correct. I was able to share what I was experiencing, listen to how they felt, and strategize together how to avoid this situation in the future. I'm always willing to be wrong (just don't tell my husband).

As observing myself in this way became a habit, I gradually found myself spotting these kinds of reactions coming on before I was overcome with emotion. Early on, when a reaction began, and I became aware of being drawn into it, I wasn't able to nip it in the bud right away. I would feel myself being triggered but I couldn't quite head it off.

This wasn't a time to criticize myself for being unable to control the reaction. This was when I patted myself on the back (and still do). I was beginning to pay attention in a new way. This is always something to feel good about, as it's a major stepping stone of our inner growth.

As the days, weeks, and months go by in my life, I continue to notice the things that trigger me and what reactions I have. As I learn how reactions get going, before long, quite out of the blue, I find myself unexpectedly intercepting the crazy train.

In my case, for months Tyler helped me pause, breathe, and calm myself. Then gradually, very gradually, came the time that, without anybody's help, I grew able to short-circuit the chain reaction that usually led to an unwelcome reaction. I wasn't able to do it perfectly; but with practice, I increasingly realized I was about to get frustrated, paused, took a deep breath, and calmed myself way, way down.

Once a reaction has been stopped in its tracks, I have an opportunity to catch a different train of thought and avoid the train wreck.

The beauty of this approach of embracing my messy state is that, instead of trying to "get rid" of an unpleasant emotion, as if something's "wrong" with what I'm feeling, awareness allows me to tap into the energy that's fueling the emotion.

As I continue to become aware of the energy that's been tangled up inside me, emotions such as anger, jealousy, or sadness are seen simply as information, rather than something "bad." Instead of trying to rid myself of the emotion, I begin to use the information it contains as a means of discovering those aspects of myself that are seeking to be recognized.

Over time, I realized I could utilize my stress as a means of uncovering the information I needed to tap into creative energy enabling me to live a more joyful, peaceful, and productive life.

What? I can welcome my stress? Yes! It always points me to where I need to focus within myself or within my life.

Learn My Triggers

Welcoming my stressed-out state may seem pretty deranged. After all, we commonly speak of someone "pressing our buttons" as a negative thing. Some people, we tell ourselves, know how to press *all* of our buttons—especially our children and our spouse—and we aren't at all amused when they do so.

In fact, we usually feel mad at the person who causes these unpleasant reactions in us. We wish they'd lay off. Of course, they rarely do. Unfortunately, personal growth doesn't consist of getting others to stop irritating us or angering us—which, if you think about it, is an impossible task anyway. Part of growth involves *discovering why we were triggered in the first place.* If no one triggered us, how would we ever grow?

Here's a different idea. Join me in welcoming frustration: Next time you are annoyed smile if you can and say, "Oh, there you are again frustration! What are you here to teach me today?" I've developed quite a relationship with my anger and frustration. We are pretty good buddies at this point and I welcome them along with me wherever I go. However, I have learned to avoid letting them lead whenever possible. I love how author Elizabeth Gilbert shares in her book *Big Magic* how her fear is always welcome with her, but it must sit in the back seat! It can't drive, change the music, or decide which direction to go. In this way, she integrates her fear and becomes more whole. I've found that banishing certain parts of myself never works. Those pieces just seem to pop up more fiercely trying to be seen.

Back in the 13th century, Jelaluddin Rumi caught the importance of welcoming all of life's experience and brought it to public attention in his poem The Guest House. Coleman Burke offers us a beautiful translation of Rumi's writing. He wrote:

This being human is a guest house.

Every morning a new arrival.

A joy, a depression, a meanness,

some momentary awareness comes

as an unexpected visitor.

Welcome and entertain them all!

Even if they are a crowd of sorrows,

who violently sweep your house

empty of its furniture,

still, treat each guest honorably.

He may be clearing you out

for some new delight.

The dark thought, the shame, the malice.

meet them at the door laughing and invite them in.

Be grateful for whatever comes.

because each has been sent

as a guide from beyond.

We *need* provocations in our life because, as Rumi shows, they are important keys to finding precious moments of inner peace.

Becoming skilled at discerning the triggers for my reactions, the things that set me off, is what finally equipped me to make changes. My growing ability to short-circuit a reaction afforded me the space to figure out what was setting me off—what, in me, was craving my attention.

I personally discovered that very often my anxiety manifested itself in the worry of running out of time. I hated being late, and my anxiety around tardiness revealed itself in my body language. When I had the thought "I might be late," this evoked in me a clenched jaw, tight throat, fast heartbeat, and overall uptight feeling.

For the record, nothing much has changed for me, other than not raising my voice in frustration when we are running out of time. I still notice the tension in my system, but I don't let it rule me these days. I share this because the reality is, this stuff doesn't necessarily go away. Sometimes it will, but in many cases we simply learn to relate to our internal reactions differently over time.

Do you know what, from my vantage point, the hardest part of parenting is? The real challenge for me of being a parent isn't dealing with the naughty or inconvenient things my children sometimes do or say. The truly difficult aspect of being an effective parent is to get *myself* under control. And there's no better place to learn this discipline than in the chaos and confusion of everyday family life. This is good news because we all have plenty of messiness to work with!

EXERCISE: EXPLORING YOUR TRIGGERS

Sit down with a journal or piece of paper and write out what triggers you most in the course of a day. Think about the morning, afternoon, and evening. Consider the home environment as well as the outside world. Which people seem to trigger an unwelcome response? What is it that they do? We can't change or make

> The real challenge for me of being a parent isn't dealing with the naughty or inconvenient things my children sometimes do or say. The truly difficult aspect of being an effective parent is to get *myself* under control.

shifts in our lives without awareness of where we struggle. Make this list without beating yourself up over any of it. Think it all through in a matter of fact way as if you were a researcher collecting data. Don't take it personally…just get to know it.

CHAPTER 3

THE FAMILY AS CATALYST FOR PERSONAL DEVELOPMENT

"We need to give up what no longer works and find new ways of being that keep us close to what matters."

– Mark Nepo

To be present as my children unfold into their uniqueness is a privilege with no equal. What my children need most of all is my presence. Committing myself to living a life filled with presence feels like a lofty goal, but one I can practice moment by moment. When I notice I'm lost in whatever is going on in or around me I always have an opportunity to start again. This feels like a worthy and doable commitment, and one I have loved to share with other parents over the years.

The family is an environment that's ideally tailored towards nurturing emotional development—not just in my children (although I will hopefully do that as well), but most especially in *myself*.

Life invites me to grow myself up alongside my growing children. This involves completing the growing up I didn't do in my own childhood. I was going to say "failed to do," but it isn't a failure. It's just part and parcel of the complex project of being a human being.

None of us is an island unto ourselves. Rather, we grow up in a family, belong to a certain society, and live at a particular time in history—all of which have a huge impact on the progress we make towards our spiritual unfolding. We aren't simply individuals, but individuals whose formation is the product of a universe of influences.

Within every interaction I have with my children lie an opportunity to shift *myself* toward a more rewarding way of living. The bonus is, that as I further my own maturity, it inevitably rubs off on my kiddos. To the degree that I'm able to school myself in a mature and wholesome approach to life, I make it easier for my children to do the same.

I've seen how, from my personal experience with my own boys as well as the many coaching clients I've worked with over the years, the kind of people our children are growing into depends greatly on the kind of people we *ourselves* are becoming. As I have learned to be a fully functional, caring, peaceful individual who radiates joy in my relationships, social life, work life, and home life, my children also have learned to be whole individuals who thrive. And on the days that I'm just worn down, grumpy, and unpleasant…well…I give myself a break and I know I can always start again later. Or maybe tomorrow. Some days are just too hard.

In other words, who *I am*—and who I am *becoming*—does more to influence my children than all of the teaching or lecturing I could ever do.

Parenting is a journey in which I am learning and growing *together* with my kiddos. Now don't get me wrong, I need to set limits, teach manners, hold my kids to expectations, and all that jazz. However, I can only do those things with authenticity if

I'm also developing mindful awareness and focusing on my own growth. You know that whole "do as I say, not as I do" thing? It just doesn't work so well for me in raising conscious children. I first have to raise myself as a conscious adult.

LEARNING TOGETHER

To give you a window into how we have grown as a family, let me share a problem that arose in our home over sleep. Anyone else ever struggle with getting kids or teens to sleep or stay asleep through the night? I'm imagining a sea of nodding heads. Glad it's not just me.

My kids have rarely in their short lives slept well. For as long as I can remember, this has been a lively topic filled with sad stories of sleepless nights. On one occasion, two mornings in a row, Tyler woke me up at 5 a.m. because he was "scared." The first morning it happened, I was sweet about it. My husband shifted into Tyler's bed downstairs, while I allowed Tyler to get into our bed.

The next morning, when we were again woken up at 5 a.m., I was less tolerant. In fact, I found myself being downright grumpy. "Go back to bed," I snapped.

When Tyler insisted on sleeping in our bed because he was frightened, I explained impatiently, "You are ten years old, which is plenty old enough to sleep by yourself. It's time you stopped looking for things to be scared of. You shouldn't wake me up. Go back to bed and go back to sleep." Having been awakened out of a deep sleep, I was in a particularly bad mood. Clearly, not one of my parenting highlights.

Later in the morning when "compassionate mommy" had returned, my son came up with a remarkable suggestion. He proposed that I do what a popular teacher called Byron Katie refers to as "The Work." He would even facilitate me in the four questions (which of course I had taught him. Here I was being played at my own game!). Astounded by his awareness, I agreed. He skillfully reminded me that I had to come up with the thought I believed was causing me to be so angry. I told him that my stressful belief was "my children shouldn't wake me up". This thought definitely caused me stress! Now he was ready to walk me through Katie's process.

The first question he asked me was, "Is it true that your children shouldn't wake you up?"

"Yes," I asserted. "My boys definitely shouldn't wake me up. It makes me grumpy all day."

"You can only answer with a 'yes' or a 'no', Mom. Which is it?"

"Okay. Yes" I responded.

Now came the second question, "Can you absolutely know it's true that we shouldn't wake you up?"

Well, of course I couldn't be *certain* the boys shouldn't wake me. What if something was really wrong? "No" I answered, begrudgingly siding with reality.

In our house, we're all quite familiar with Katie's Work, so we have a little cheat sheet where the questions are printed. Everyone knows where to find the card—and my boys happily do, especially when they are the ones in trouble. Wink, wink.

Reading from the questions, my son asked, "What happens when you believe the thought, 'My boys shouldn't wake me up'?"

I responded, "I get angry and impatient. I withhold love. I'm unkind. My body gets tight. All of which only makes things worse."

I sat in stillness for several moments, allowing the question to penetrate to a deeper level, sensing there was more to emerge. As I did so, I found myself tapping into a fear that lay beneath my grumpy state. Examining this fear, the bottom line turned out to be that I was concerned about getting my sleep. I was also worried about the boys not getting enough sleep. And, I feared that lack of sleep would cause me (and them) to be moody *all day*.

Tyler proceeded to the next question: "Who would you be without the thought, 'My boys shouldn't wake me up'?"

Of course, I knew exactly the kind of person I would be if I didn't believe that thought. "I'd be more peaceful," I admitted. "As a result, I would be empathetic, which would mean I could offer constructive help in this situation. And since I would be able to remain calm, I wouldn't end up beating myself up later for getting mad at you. As for having been woken early, I'd just be 'a woman who was woken up,' with no story in my head about how awful it is to be woken prematurely."

We now moved to the fourth question, as Tyler inquired, "Can you turn it around and tell me the opposite of your stressful thought "My boys shouldn't wake me up"?

I could indeed, and I actually made *two* turnarounds. "Tyler should wake me up if he needs to," I first realized. Then I gave three examples of why he should wake me: if he was scared, if he didn't feel he could be alone in his room at this moment, and if he needed my support. After all, as his mother, wasn't it my job to support him emotionally in the face of the fear he was experiencing?

The second turnaround surprised me. "I should wake *myself* up," I found myself saying, without at first realizing quite what

I was uncovering in myself. It turned out that I wasn't referring to waking up from physical slumber. Rather, a deeper awakening emerged that involved waking myself up from the negative thoughts that overpowered me as a result of all the things I told myself about being shortchanged on family sleep. Such thoughts were cutting me off from my innate good nature.

It was becoming apparent that when my boys woke me, I could use it as a cue to usher myself into a deeper awareness. The whole episode of being *physically* awakened two mornings in a row was here to propel me into *inner* growth.

As I explained my insight to Tyler, he commented, "Good work, Mom." Then he probed, "How do you feel now?"

"I feel much better," I assured him. "Thank you for walking me through the questions." In my heart, I bowed to what an incredible teacher he is for me.

Use Your Head, Don't Lose It

As I touched on in the previous chapter, if we *lose* our head in an emotional reaction, we can't *use* our head in a creative way for problem solving. And let's face it, parenting involves solving one apparent problem after another—it's in the DNA.

Once I had broken out of my story about how unfair it was to be awakened early, I was able to become a skillful listener and understand why Tyler was awakening early. I finally had the information I needed to help my little guy.

Together, we came up with a solution—one that, by being deeply heard, Tyler *himself* was able to suggest. This is the ideal in parenting—empowering our children to come up with their own answers and gain the skill to find solutions in their own lives.

———

And so he came up with his own solution. He asked me to buy him homeopathic calming drops, the kind designed especially for children. I had forgotten we'd used these successfully in the past. He would keep these by his bedside and take them each night. Just like that, for the time being at least, he not only had solved his own problem but also helped facilitate his mother's inner growth. I'll chalk that up as a good day.

As long as we parents are caught up in an emotional reaction, we really can't be helpful to our children—or to anyone else, for that matter. The effect of anger is constriction, shutting down our ability to think creatively. In the presence of the chemicals that course through our system when we are in this state, imaginative solutions elude us.

Rather than placing all the attention on the child as the "problem" when situations arise in the family, if we can focus on ourselves first, the home becomes a catalyst for growth. Parent and child help each other grow up together.

PRACTICING MEDITATION

Meditation offers us the ability to know ourselves better. Even five minutes a day on a regular basis can help us learn how to be more aware of our thoughts, emotions, and feelings. Starting small and working up to longer meditation sessions is perfectly reasonable. If you do not have a regular meditation practice but would like to start one I can suggest some resources. The Mindful Schools has a wonderful online class

> Rather than placing all the attention on the child as the "problem" when situations arise in the family, if we can focus on ourselves first, the home becomes a catalyst for growth. Parent and child help each other grow up together.

called Mindfulness Fundamentals; www.Headspace.com is a great resource, Insight Timer and Simple Habit are wonderful apps that offers free guided meditations (including some from me) and ways to time your practice. You can go to my website michel-legale.com and join my community to receive "A Busy Parents Guide to Practicing Mindfulness" which includes free meditations written specifically for parents. You can also sign up to listen to my Podcast called (what else) but "Mindful Parenting in a Messy World".

CHAPTER 4

AWARENESS ENTERS THE PICTURE

"To become mindful...present...is really the invitation to work with the joys and sorrows of the world, and to do so with this gift, this capacity of loving awareness, of attention that actually can be present for the whole dance."

- Jack Kornfield

WHEN MY CHILDREN were born, I hadn't yet landed on what was to become my path of inner growth. There were lots of pointers toward it, and each one had led me closer and closer to the time that I would begin practicing mindful awareness on a regular basis, finding greater peace within myself and in my life.

The first sign of things to come came in my college days, when someone handed me a book by Thich Nhat Hahn called "Peace is Every Step: The Path of Mindfulness in Every Day Life." It was the first time I realized that Catholicism wasn't my only option for spiritual growth. It seems silly now, but at the time it pretty much blew my mind. I devoured the words from cover to cover. I began to think about and see my life differently for the first time. I had honestly never given much thought to actively cultivating peace in my life, nor in studying my own thoughts as Thich Nhat Hahn was suggesting. In reading this one book, the seeds of change within me had officially began to grow.

Maya Angelou, an American poet, author, and civil rights activist is one of my heroes and really influenced me during my college years. I was interested in reading biographies written by powerful women and Maya's seven autobiographies kept me busy reading late into the night. Even though my life was so different from Angelou's, I resonated with the way she had been through hell and come out the other side shining in such a bright way. She had known poverty, suffered abuse, and was a black woman at a time when it was even more difficult simply to be a woman. Yet, she was a remarkable example of resilience. Up until my college years, I hadn't really thought much about using the difficult situations from my past and present as invitations to personal development. I framed her poem *And Still I Rise* to remind me that no matter what life sends our way, and how bad things get, we can still move forward. Her story was my story.

A Different Way to Approach Everyday Life

Another book came into my life around the same time as Maya Angelou's and Thich Nhat Hanh's, again quite inadvertently through a friend. *The Tao of Pooh* not only made me smile, it introduced me to the Tao Te Ching and the importance of allowing life to simply unfold while practicing the act of being with life "as it is," moment by moment. This does not mean that we don't need to work on ourselves, but it is important to recognize and trust our own inner nature. The more awareness we gather about who we are, the easier it is to meet the moments of our lives with kindness and understanding. I loved the concept of trusting life. It was fundamentally different from the anxious way I had always known myself to be until that point. I just didn't have a clue how to put it into practice. How *does* one just "go with the flow" and trust our inner nature?

This answer to this question was to become especially important years later when I married and we began a family of our own. How does one "go with the flow" amid piles of washing, screaming kids, the need to get dinner on the table, and work to finish for the office the next morning? Life was taking me on a journey that would show me how this is possible.

While working in New York for the summer during my college years, I walked into a bookstore in Soho. Quite out of the blue, a man asked me, "Have you ever read this? It's one of my favorites."

The book was *The Alchemist*. Though I was staying with friends, intent on exploring New York during my school break, I found myself delving into this book that had come to me at the suggestion of a total stranger. The story tells of an Egyptian shepherd boy who dreams of finding treasure. When he sets off in search of it, he ends up discovering that the only true treasure is to be found somewhere we are already familiar with—in the depths of our own being.

As I read, I resonated with the idea of a profound meaning to life that's rooted in our depths. I also suspected that many of us are closed off to awareness of this deeper sense of ourselves. Slowly beginning this exploration of my inner world, I suspected I had been living one of those half-lives. Absorbing the book's message, I sensed there's more to life than simply going through the motions of everyday routines. I was beginning to get a clue as to what Winnie the Pooh so clearly understood about his and others own true nature.

Just as the story of the Alchemist unfolded, I began to be aware of a hidden dimension in me that, once discovered, brought a serious sparkle into my daily experience. Simply as a result of becoming aware of this about myself, so much more became meaningful. I can tell you from experience that this shift can make for a spectacular life.

After I had children, at some point it became apparent to me that awareness of our deeper self is the missing element in how we raise our families. It's what transforms diapers, curfews, and dishes from drudgery into a journey of self-discovery and self-development.

Jon Kabat-Zinn defines mindfulness as: "The awareness that emerges through paying attention on purpose, in the present moment, and non-judgmentally to the unfolding of experience moment by moment." After hearing this quote for the first time I really connected to the idea of not judging my experience. Observing our thoughts and emotions with a curiosity rather than a criticism is a key aspect of practice. At first I was horrified, listening to the inner critic living within me, but over time I learned to hear that voice and not take her so seriously. Who says we have to believe everything we think? I don't recommend it.

> After I had children, at some point it became apparent to me that awareness of our deeper self is the missing element in how we raise our families. It's what transforms diapers, curfews, and dishes from drudgery into a journey of self-discovery and self-development.

My dear friend and teacher Mark Coleman defines mindfulness as "clear present moment awareness of inner and outer experience that nurtures a wise, caring response to life". I love this definition because it oozes empowerment to me. I feel better and stronger when I respond to life circumstances in a wise and caring way.

This practice of mindfulness would ultimately become my path to healing, although it would come slowly at first. What I knew for sure quite early on in parenthood was that my children came into my life not only for their growth, but also for mine. They have the capacity to awaken me to the fact that I have deeper layers within myself, yet to be uncovered. Mindful awareness helps me to discover precisely where and how I have yet to grow day by day.

PRACTICE:

Practicing Self-Observation

Self-Observation is crucial to getting to know ourselves and creating any kind of lasting change.

Choose one of your triggers and spend the next week observing yourself. During this time, you are not trying to change anything about your behavior. Simply get curious. Pause when you notice your trigger. Make note of your current situation, any emotions that are present, body sensations, or thoughts you are having. You can journal right away if that is available to you, otherwise journal each evening. It is often the case that simply bringing awareness to a difficulty in our life can shift it, but sometimes we need outside help with a coach, therapist, or dear friend.

Chapter 5

Finding Meditation

"Nurturing your own development isn't selfish. It's actually a great gift to give to other people. "

– Rick Hanson

WHAT I DIDN'T REALIZE when awareness began to take center stage in my life is that you don't get far on a trajectory of self-discovery and self-development without elements of your past being stirred up so you can address them. I would discover that life has surprising ways of bringing these things to our attention. Ouch.

During my college years, I found myself quite lost and fairly self-destructive. Don't get me wrong, I was incredibly responsible in that I paid my own way through college and worked full time doing it. However, I carried with me a lot of pain, confusion, and loneliness that I numbed through alcohol, sedatives, drugs, and bad relationships with men for a long time. It's unclear how I managed to get good grades while rolling out of a club at 8am and then right into a class tripping on acid or high on ecstasy. At one point, I went so far as to date and live with a drug dealer. I thank my lucky stars he was never arrested while we were together. I would have likely ended up in prison alongside him.

One weekend, when my life felt particularly out of control, I decided to attend service at Unity church. I have no idea how or where I got the idea to attend, but for some unknown reason to me, I found myself sitting there during a Sunday service surrounded by people of all religious denominations. Each Sunday they led a thirty-minute guided meditation and during this time I found myself holding the hands of strangers next to me and pouring tears. It was my first experience with meditation and it shook me to my core. I had no idea what these tears were about, but obviously *something* within me needed my attention. But what? I was puzzled by the tears that came so freely during church service and I began to get curious about what was being woken up inside of me. I was officially beginning to practice was I was learning about in the many books I had been reading.

The pressure of working to put myself through school, coupled with the crazy belief that I wasn't particularly smart, evoked a great deal of anxiety in me. Whether it involved paying bills, dealing with my family situation back home, or having an awareness of my limitations, my entire system reeked of worry. A cloud of doom seemed to hover over me all the time.

It was the late 80s and early 90s, and the era of the cassette tape. I bought a series of meditations in the church store to use at bedtime. Slowly, the meditations began to have an impact and, surprisingly, I found my anxiety starting to ease up a little bit. It would be a long time until I would make a lifelong commitment to a meditation practice but the seeds had been planted.

A large part of my anxiety appeared to come from a concern about whether I "belonged." Just to be "me" felt extremely uncomfortable, since I didn't really know who "me" was. I lived at the surface of who I was, probably because what lurked underneath hurt. As I look back now it's pretty clear that my hidden emotions and feelings lived right behind my worry about not belonging. It's no surprise that the ecstasy drug culture in my college town appealed so much to me for so long. When we were all high on ecstasy it felt like we all belonged to each other. I experienced this as pure bliss. I realize now that it wasn't whether I fit in or not, but that I was uneasy about who I thought I was as a human being. I beat myself up for many years embarrassed that I was so caught up in doing ecstasy. I wish I could say it was a once and awhile thing. For a couple of years, I did it several times a week and took way more pills in one evening than were even close to being safe for my size. I felt ashamed that I had been so emotionally addicted to this drug. To this day, I can't even hear house music without getting a stomach ache. However, when I think back to that time now, I have nothing but compassion for the young woman I used to be. She was longing for deep connection with herself and others…she just didn't have the capacity yet within herself to make those longings a reality. Those hours that she was high and feeling connected actually helped her learn what was possible. I'm sending a shout out to my best friend Katie who took many calls those evenings in the middle of the night when the drugs would begin to wear off and I needed to connect with someone who knew me and loved me. Deep connections were available all along if I only looked in the right place.

"Me, Spiritual?"

Though I listened to guided meditations as well as engaged in meditations at church during college, I had never previously thought of myself as a spiritual person. In my teens, I found myself rebelling against the Catholic faith I had been raised in.

It all came to a head at age fourteen when my mother insisted I go through the ritual of confirmation. "What if you want to marry someone who's Catholic?" she argued when I objected. "If your future husband wants to get married in a church, you *have* to be confirmed." My stubborn teen self-assured her that I would never be married in a Catholic Church. For the record, I was married at a vineyard in Northern California. Apparently, my teen self knew me pretty well.

I decided to go through with the confirmation to make my mother happy. However, during the excruciatingly long process of being confirmed, my mother attended a parent meeting, learning the rules for confirmation. A deacon told the group of parents that, "Every child needs a sponsor." Then he made the mistake of informing my mother that a parent *could not* be a sponsor… unless the child happened to be adopted. The implication was, of course, that a parent of an adopted child wasn't *really* the child's parent, and could thus function as her sponsor. Stay with me here. Considering that I was adopted, my mother was infuriated and told the deacon so in less-than-loving and quite creative language. She also told me what he had said, which drove me from token rebellion against Catholicism to utter repulsion. I gritted my teeth all the way through my confirmation.

I've come to see there are lots of silly rules in religion. I've also come to learn that formal religion can be a beautiful thing for certain people and I deeply respect all of those who follow this path, it just didn't happen to be for me. It's none of my business or concern what religion anyone else practices, other than to honor their views and beliefs. All that ever matters is that I personally feel aligned with my own path of inner growth. We all have our own needs in any given moment during any given lifetime.

Back in college, when the various pointers of my need for a spiritual dimension to my life began appearing, I finally began to think about what I believed, rather than what I was told growing up. But I was thinking in the context of spirituality instead of religion. I had no idea you could be spiritual but not religious, a phenomenon that's becoming common today in the United States as so eloquently shared in Roger Housden's beautifully written book on the subject, *Keeping the Faith Without a Religion*.

I love a quote by the Dalai Lama that says, "My religion is very simple. My religion is kindness." Striving each day to be kind to myself and kind to others sounds about right to me.

BRING ON THOSE QUESTIONS!

I now found myself as a curious college student questioning everything, and open to ideas I had never considered. For instance, as a Catholic, I hadn't thought about reincarnation. But when someone gave me Brian Weiss' *Many Lives, Many Masters*, which is the true story of a prominent psychiatrist, his young patient, and the past-life therapy that changed both of their lives, I didn't automatically reject the idea because it was different from what I'd been taught. On the contrary, I stayed up late at night devouring it and found myself left with even more curiosity.

Though I had no clue about reincarnation when I was first handed the book, the idea that the soul's journey might be different from what my faith had taught me was fascinating. The deeper I dug, the more sense it made that we are involved in a soul journey that extends far beyond this present life. At least, this is what makes the most sense to me so far, as I type these words. The reality is that none of us knows for sure and it's perfectly fine for our beliefs to evolve over time—or not.

This was the first time I felt connected to the idea of myself as a soul on a journey. It had never dawned on me that this life could be just one tiny sliver in an infinite experience. That there might be something important for me to learn from my present life—something specific to *me,* a karmic reason I had come into the world—somehow resonated with me. Could understanding karma help me embrace my messy life? Clearly, some exploration was in order.

Exploring karma led me to exploring my soul. To be a soul—to be pure consciousness in my deepest being—means I have a calm center that can never be shaken by the mess life can sometimes hand me, whether in my parenting dynamic or otherwise.

Perhaps you don't think of yourself as a soul. I happen to like the word soul, though terms like spirit, higher self, true self, or the divine image and likeness are all fine. Whatever floats your boat really—the exact expression isn't important. It's the awareness of myself as more than I ever imagined myself to be that really matters. This is yummy deep stuff.

Embracing the Terror of Silence

I mentioned how the guided meditations I participated in during college reduced my anxiety level. As I began to find ease in sitting in stillness I found myself sleeping better and feeling more grounded. I had no idea I was living in an anxious fog all of those years prior.

Though I now found I could relax somewhat at night, I was still extremely anxious much of the day. Carrying the relaxation

I experienced at night into my waking life was something I still had no clue how to do. I wanted to "go with the flow" in the way I'd read about in *The Tao of Pooh*, but crippling anxiety and going with the flow don't mesh. I was determined to have other options to manage my anxiety than stealing my grandmothers Xanax when I was home from college. For a few years during college, I took chips of Xanax throughout the day just to get through life without feeling like my insides were going to explode. My personal brand of anxiety has always been very body focused. From the time I was teenager until this very day, if I'm anxious I feel it in my belly and in the tightness of my chest. If only my adult self could have whispered to my teen self and pointed me towards meditation and awareness-based practices much sooner. But then I wouldn't have this book to write now would I?

Personal discovery and self-development have not come as lightning bolts from the sky for me. Oh, I may have insightful moments that catapult me forward, but generally it's been a process that's undergone step by step, one insight and experience building upon another.

Life had to gradually prepare me for the deeper self-awareness that would come when I made a shift from guided meditation to sitting in stillness, simply with myself—a shift that wouldn't come until after having two children.

When I first tried sitting in silence for twenty minutes, you can't imagine how much it shocked my system—I'll never forget it. At the time, I was in a year long program, training to be a coach with New Venture West in San Francisco. Meditation was one of the requirements of the training and I showed up as a willing student. Since I had done guided meditations back in college,

I thought I could meditate and would be okay with just sitting in silence. How hard could it be, right?

I sat through the guided section of the meditation comfortably. However, once everything went quiet, it wasn't long before I experienced such discomfort that I thought I would implode. Seriously, I wanted to scream and run out of the room. My chest felt tight, I could barely breathe, and my stomach turned in sickness. I had never sat in quiet stillness like this for any length of time. Consequently, I hadn't paid attention to the drama playing out in my mind either. In fact, it became painfully obvious that I had done everything I could do to avoid tuning into it. Now, unable to tune it out by staying busy, listening to music, or any of the other things I latch onto in order to escape paying attention to myself, I was forced to sit in unbearable discomfort.

Simply sitting in stillness and silence—with no guided meditation, no yoga poses to keep my mind busy—was so jarring, it forced me to face the fact that I had way more work to do on myself than I even imagined. I thought of the cleansing tears that had fallen from my eyes during my first experience with meditation at Unity Church. Here I found myself, over twelve years and two children later, having that same familiar realization that something deep inside of me needed tending to. Here we go again I thought. This is pretty much how it is. One minute we think we are shuffling along through life just fine and the next...WHAM. Welcome to your next challenge as a human being.

I was determined to sit in meditation without freaking out. I started

> One minute we think we are shuffling along through life just fine and the next...WHAM. Welcome to your next challenge as a human being.

by sitting for five minutes at a time, eventually building up to twenty minutes. Though I still found myself thinking from time to time about how easily xanax or valium had calmed my inner insanity, these mindful moments initiated my ability to manage my anxiety on my own. Freedom is possible after all.

Meditation became a staple in my life. No longer locked in constant thought or emotional reactivity, I began discovering what it is to simply be *aware*. During my year in coaching school, practicing awareness became a central feature of my life and continues today.

FINDING THE TIME FOR MEDITATION

Having a family made it challenging to make space for a regular time of stillness in the day. This was especially the case when I was working or had other responsibilities that took me out of the home for long hours. This is when "working with what I've got" was most helpful.

If you're a parent, you know that little ones don't always just climb into bed and go to sleep when we might like them to. Periodically through the years, my boys would have a hard time going to sleep unless I remained in their room. It wasn't just for a few minutes that they needed me with them, but until they fell asleep. Consequently, my meditation practice suffered, as evenings were often the only quiet time I could find for myself. I have to smile at how I had gone from wanting to run from stillness to craving it—and resenting the fact that I struggled to make time for it in my daily routine!

When I shared this problem with one of my teachers, Wendy Palmer, she suggested I bring my meditation cushion into the

boys' room and sit until they
fell asleep. What an ingenious
idea! When I approached
my boys with this idea, they
wanted to give it a try. We ne-
gotiated an agreement that, as
long as this remained a quiet
time for all of us, I would en-
gage in my meditation practice while they went to sleep.

So each night we would have our cuddle time, our ritual time,
and then I would plop myself on my cushion as they fell into their
sleep. Like magic, we all got what we needed. The solution was
staring me in the face once I slowed down enough to look for it.
For the record, I still lay in bed with my youngest son as he falls
asleep and generally fall asleep myself. I end up going to bed early,
which allows me to wake up early, and practice meditation while
the house is still quiet. I like to think my children have been at the
center of how I find time to practice, rather than being between
me and my practice.

When I had children, life didn't come wrapped up in neat
packages. As a parent, I couldn't take too seriously the common
meditation instructions that said, "Sit at the same time and same
place each day." In a parent's world, you take it where you can get
it. Though I aspired to meditate for at least forty minutes a day, I
often found ten minutes (or two minutes) just had to do. A little
meditation practice is better than no meditation practice.

Back in those days, in addition to meditating on a daily basis
for whatever length of time I could muster, I attended day-long

and weekend retreats whenever I could. I also spent countless "mommy" days exploring things like the enneagram, energy healing, and studying just about anything that had to do with understanding my mind. I've always been drawn to studying Buddhism because the Buddha feels to me like a scientist. He systematically studied the mind, the body, and ways of being in the world.

Another meditation tip I can share that works for me is to always leave a scarf, sweater, and/or wrap near the bed. If I wake up during the night or too early in the morning, I put these on to stay warm, then sit myself up on my pillow as if it were my meditation cushion. Sometimes I go back to sleep after sitting for a while. Other times, I just stay where I am in silence until my children or husband wake me up.

> Once I stopped trying to force my vision of "perfection" onto situations in my life, solutions found a way of appearing. Another reminder to embrace the mess.

For many years I experienced myself as a total fraud meditation practitioner because I had not yet been away on extended retreats. But that turned out to be total crazy talk by me! I came to regular practice as a parent, and us parents know darn well that we need to get things done *creatively*. Always. I pieced together my mindfulness and meditation practices over the years in any way I could. This made me a hero, not a fraud!

Once I stopped trying to force my vision of "perfection" onto situations in my life, solutions found a way of appearing. Another reminder to embrace the mess.

JOURNAL

What is your relationship to spirituality and religion? There is no right or wrong answer. Think back to your childhood, adolescence, and young adulthood. How did your beliefs about spirituality or religion take shape? How have your beliefs evolved over time and what encouraged this evolution?

CHAPTER 6

SEARCHING FOR OUR TRUE SELF

"Happiness lies not in finding what is missing, but in finding what is present."

– Tara Brach

I WORK WITH SO MANY clients who say, "I can't be myself around such and such a person." Or they may say, "Whenever I get close to someone, I lose myself in the relationship." Sound familiar?

The problem in these cases is often the need to reconnect with a sense of self. Young children who haven't had any major trauma have no problem with this stuff by the way. They are so close to the divine within themselves it doesn't even dawn on them that they are not connected.

One of the keys I've found to living a fulfilling life is to know where I end and others begin. It's magical, learning to be close to others, yet be entirely my own person. In psychological terms, it's called differentiation and it's one of the developmental milestones which leads to a healthy emotional life.

When we are secure individuals we avoid twisting ourselves into someone we're not. We don't need to distance ourselves from others in order to feel "safe." We can stand up for ourselves calmly, unapologetically, unreservedly, all the while remaining closely connected. Does this sound dreamy or what?

My intention is always to maintain an even keel emotionally, even if an emotional storm is raging around me. When I'm knocked off center as easily as the wind blows my days don't run so smoothly. I know I'm standing strong within myself when I no longer say things like, "You're making me angry" or the dreaded "How could you do this to me?" *I* am in charge of my responses to people and situations. I'm not particularly interested in being an emotional puppet, dancing to another's whims.

Since the art of being true to myself wasn't taught in school, it has to be learned the messy way—in the school of daily life where I have the opportunity to learn about myself more and more each day. It's the essence of what a mindful life journey is all about. Paying attention on purpose is the best way I know how to get to know the inner workings of my mind, heart, and spirit. I've learned to hang on tight for the bumpy ride and make the most of each moment whenever I can.

Lost to Ourselves, We Borrow an Identity

Unfortunately, we all have to recover from our childhood in one way or another. Even the greatest of parents can't meet every need their children have.

If we didn't learn emotional independence in our childhood home, raising our own children becomes our opportunity to do so. Kids trigger our emotional immaturity in the same way we triggered our parents, but just had no idea we were doing it.

From generation to generation—in our homes, places of business, social institutions, and communities—we go through life reacting in ways that are often destructive. Lacking a strong sense of self, we miss out on the opportunity to respond to each other in fresh, insightful, creative ways that promote understanding.

As I entered my teens, I thought I had a pretty clear sense of myself and what my life ought to be like. Don't we all?

I grew up in Long Island and did relatively well in school until ninth grade. Only then did things start getting more difficult for me academically. I honestly didn't care about academics because my passion in life was dancing. In my brilliant young mind, I decided I was either going to perform on Broadway or would own my own dance school. Those were the only two paths I saw for myself. I knew I probably needed to have my high school diploma in case I wanted to study somewhere like Juilliard so I did enough to pass my classes, but my education was of very little interest to me at that point.

When I was in seventh grade, the dance school I attended wanted me to take more classes. I was already taking five or six a week, and my mom couldn't afford to sign me up for more. The school and I worked out a trade, and I began teaching the younger students, something I did for the next few years. When I wasn't dancing either as a student or a teacher, you could find me making up new dance routines in my garage. I was completely focused.

Dancing wasn't my only interest. I also played sports and rode horses competitively for several years. As I look back now, I understand what the magic was for me in these activities, though I couldn't have articulated it at the time. Whenever I danced, performed gymnastics, or played a sport, I felt myself to be in what author Mihaly Csikszentmihali describes as *flow* in his book titled FLOW, The Psychology of Optimal Experience. I would regularly have moments of ease where the moves came naturally.

For instance, whenever I rode a horse, it truly felt as if the horse and I were one with the environment around us. I was experiencing what was described in *The Tao of Pooh*. Pooh doesn't hesitate, calculate, or pontificate. He just *is*.

I experienced flow through these many activities until we left Long Island and moved to Florida when I was in tenth grade. As you can imagine, moving in the middle of high school and leaving all of my personal interests that kept me incredibly grounded was quite challenging for me. Overnight, all of the activities that brought me joy were no longer available to me. Before moving, I wasn't the best student, but I wasn't the worst either. You could say I was getting by. After moving, I quickly became completely disengaged from my academics and barely made it through high school. I remember waiting anxiously to see if I had scraped through oceanography with a C grade so I could walk across the platform and graduate with my friends. If you would have told me then that I ultimately would make it through graduate school, well into my forties, studying psychology, I would not have believed it possible.

Being so young, I didn't realize how much the dance school I had attended in New York had meant to me. This place helped me feel that I truly belonged. It assisted me in experiencing a strong sense of myself that was intimately connected to others. This was what I looked to create during my college years on ecstasy. I wanted to feel connected to something. Anything. Being a part of my dancing school community felt like home to me. It stayed in my memory and offered me a preview of what it would feel like to "come home to myself" someday much later on in my life.

Why We Feel Lost

Why did I gravitate so strongly to the dance school and other forms of physical activity? I suspect these things grounded me in a way I couldn't do on my own.

I didn't have a terrible childhood. I experienced safety and love, and appreciate deeply the life my parents made possible for me. But the truth is, it was a struggle for me as a nine-year-old girl and then teenager, to live through a tumultuous divorce. Although those were difficult times, in recent years I've come to realize that even through all the upheaval of my family life, everyone did their best with what they had to work with. It was precisely these difficult experiences that would prompt me to focus on healing myself many years later. It was all meant perfectly for me.

Despite my parents' commitment to me, we constantly struggled with each other over the years. Much of the time things felt "out of place" in my life. The result was that I found myself constantly challenged to feel connected within my immediate family, regardless of how much I knew I was loved.

Today, I recognize that my mom and I were like Siamese twins, joined at the hip emotionally. Two heads and one body. Our struggles often could be found in who was trying to be in control from moment to moment. Both anxious, both easily upset, we played into one another's drama, spending too much time reacting to each other. We laughed hard at times, but fought even harder.

After my parents divorced I only saw my father on the weekends after having him as the center of my world when he lived at home. Finding peace within these core relationships in my life has always been elusive to me. However, I know now unequivocally that the answer lies in finding peace within myself.

Isn't this the case in so many homes? People distance each other and live parallel lives without deep connection, or they repeatedly lock horns with each other. In my case, these two polarities played out separately with each of my parents.

I locked horns with my mom and felt distant from my dad, never feeling as connected and secure as I wanted or needed . Fast forward to today and what I notice is how these memories and fears of not being connected show up in my relationship with my own children. On more than one occasion I have found myself daydreaming about not having a close relationship with my kids after they left for college. It generally doesn't take long until I snap myself out of dreamland, come back to the present, and see what is right in front of me: children who I adore and share a beautiful relationship with. I know without a doubt that the relationship with my children is part of my own childhood healing, and that is a true blessing. Within the parent-child relationship, we have the opportunity to cultivate deep connection while also healing our past.

I have to watch closely not to repeat patterns of behavior, but instead stay wide-awake to living with awareness.

The "Glass Is Half Full" Girl

The one element I most needed as a young girl was to feel good about myself *internally.* I needed to get a sense of my true worth, valuable *in and of itself,* quite apart from anything I may be capable of or accomplish. When I wasn't able to identify internally with my true worth, like everyone else I developed a variety of personas. In psychological terms, a persona is something we project out to the world and wear like a mask. It's the part of our personality we let others see while we hide who we really are.

One of the main personas I took on after my parents' divorce was that of a "positive" person. In fact, my mother used to refer to me as her "glass is half full" daughter. I always tried to see the bright side of everything.

> Within the parent-child relationship, we have the opportunity to cultivate deep connection while also healing our past.

Why did I choose to see the bright side? To be the "glass is half full" girl was my way of making everything okay when it really wasn't. It was a way of hiding from how empty I felt inside. During the years I engaged in physical activity such as dancing, athletics, and horse riding, my focus on these things compensated for how empty and scared I often felt. Yes, I loved these activities and they helped me experience myself as more whole, but they also played a critical role in keeping me happy when I might have otherwise been depressed and melancholy.

The pain most families experience isn't evident to the outside world. After my parents divorced, I remember feeling sad about the way they were always fighting. I hated the drama. I've since learned through my coaching practice and countless conversations with parents who have kids that live with these kinds of feelings every day. It's difficult for families to know how to connect closely while simultaneously promoting the individuality of the various members of the family.

The more in touch I've become with the ways in which my own childhood enriched me, and yet failed to help me connect to a solid sense of myself, the more I've been able to support each of my own children in becoming the unique individuals they are meant to be. I needed to do this exploration within myself before I could even begin to expect to offer my children what they truly needed from me, which is to stand in their presence with all of my personas sitting on the sideline. When I'm at home with myself they have no need to borrow an identity. My work is to continue with my inner journey and knowing, so they can grow into their own beautifully differentiated selves. I need to continue to get out of my own way…and theirs.

Persona Play

Sit down with a piece of paper and something to write with. I like to use multiple colors for fun but anything you have available is fine. In the center of the paper write the word "true self" and circle it. Now, start to think of all the personas or masks you wear throughout the day. Some of my personas include: nurturer, mindful momma, mischievous competitor, creative gal, dictator, coach, impatient rabbit, helper. You get the idea. Have fun with this. Most people I work with can name at least fifteen and often many more. Once you get them on paper reflect on when this persona began in your life. Was it childhood? As a teen? During college? Why did it emerge? This is simply an exercise in self-discovery. Once you are aware of your personas you have more choice as to if or when they show themselves. Is it possible that some of your personas are ready to be released? Which ones are you most attached to?

CHAPTER 7

HOW HAVING A FAMILY OF MY OWN GREW ME UP

"When we begin to know ourselves in an open and supportive way, we take the first step to encourage our children to know themselves."

– Dan Siegel

CHILDREN PICK UP the vibes we put out. Do you know what lurks in nearly every family in America? Even the happy ones? Fear.

Although I may try to hide my fears, the feelings come across and my kiddos pick up on them anyway. They pick them up even when I'm not aware of those fears. In fact, I would guess that a lot of what we learn as children comes not from what our parents or other authority figures try to teach us, but from the unconscious energies that flood our time together in a similar way to how unheard and unseen radio waves or cell phone signals flood our homes.

When I get clear on what I'm afraid of, particularly in the parent child dynamic, I actually have a chance at putting those fears aside. I certainly prefer to be with life as it really is, rather than looking through the lens of my fears. Who doesn't struggle with fear and worry where our children are concerned? How could we not? Are they OK socially, will they be good enough to make the team, will they get into a good college, are they going to come home to visit after moving out?

What is important to remember, is that under all of this fear and worry lie OUR insecurities. Not our children's. OURS. Yes, we will support them and love them through every single phase of their lives, but our fear and anxiety does little for them. To be honest, it usually makes them recoil from us because they have no idea what we are so worried about most of the time. Our children's ability to live in the moment is simply an invitation to join them there.

LET THE UNIVERSE WORK WITH YOU

Whenever our children trigger our anxiety, they actually do us a favor. No really, stay with me here. They may send us into orbit from time to time, but their tormenting of us is precisely what we need.

When I allow myself to learn from my children, they generously guide me towards emotional growth. As I face up to my immature outbursts, my inclination to be a neat freak, or my insistence on not being a second late, by calming myself instead of exploding—addressing my children patiently and kindly rather than as a maniac on a mission to get something done—I grow in ways I never could have imagined before becoming a mother.

As I discussed in an earlier chapter, the key for me was to learn to stop myself as I'm about to react, tune into what's really driving the emotion I'm experiencing, and settle myself down. It's so clear to me that my children, with all the chaos they bring with them, have come into my life to give me a wealth of practice at this!

However, if it wasn't for my meditation and mindfulness practices it would be really difficult for me to notice my big emotions and tune in to my negative reactions before they get going.

I never underestimate the universe's wisdom. I've learned that when it looks like things are careening out of control and the very worst is happening, divine wisdom is right in the thick of it all. The messier the situation, the greater the potential to become more aware. This is good news because the mess is at times everywhere.

And speaking of messy, thinking back to the time when my hormones were kicking in, propelling me into all the drama that tends to accompany the teen years, my mother entered upon her own heightened drama in the form of menopause. Could there be a worse mix? You can imagine how this made for a particularly trying time.

You might be tempted to conclude it was bad timing on the part of nature to organize *both* our lives around the two pinnacles of hormonal activity in a woman's time on earth simultaneously. Couldn't one of us have gotten through this momentous episode before the other also embarked on such a dramatic change?

> I've learned that when it looks like things are careening out of control and the very worst is happening, divine wisdom is right in the thick of it all.

While many people think of living mindfully as something other than the messiness of daily existence, I've come to see that it's precisely in the messiness that mindfulness is forged. The mess isn't to be sidestepped or escaped, but to be plunged into with zest. *Into* the mess, embracing the entirety of it, is the direction of the mindful journey, not detouring around or away from it, as we are so easily drawn to do. Mindfulness isn't about avoiding life's chaos, but about learning to embrace the complexity in such a way that we are enriched by it instead of just reacting to it. OK, so the enrichment part sometimes takes time to realize but it always seems to arrive at some point! Let's just promise each other we will stay with it.

As I got to know myself better and years after my mom and I struggled with our hormones, I eventually came to see that she and I going through earthshaking changes concurrently was no mere fluke. It was a *setup*—a mighty *upsetting* one at that. We struggled together almost daily. However, that whole situation played an important role in me becoming the person I know myself to be today. At that time, my mom and I were not able to regulate ourselves and often blamed each other for not understanding the others perspectives. In looking back now I can imagine the possibility of the two of us listening deeply to what the other was going through and connecting rather than arguing.

The Mess is Where Awareness Really Happens

How do dirty diapers, squabbling siblings, and kids who refuse to go to sleep when we are exhausted enrich us—particularly when, if you're a woman, you might be in the throes of PMS? I'll admit that sometimes all bets are off if I have PMS. We can do hard things, but not always that hard.

Practicing mindfulness involves recognizing that life in a family is a setup for *our* learning as parents, and only secondarily for that of our children or partner. Of course, there's learning to be had on their part, but this can't be our focus when we're seeking to grow. The path of self-development requires us to detect the setup in all the myriad situations that invite a reaction from us.

Whenever I feel upset by something, I know that I'm being set up to grow. When someone says something about me that seems so wrong, or does something really irritating, the challenge is to try and identify with even the one or two percent of what they say that's spot on, so that I have the opportunity to learn from them. If there wasn't learning to be had, I wouldn't be reacting. *Any* level of reaction points to an emotional charge that is worth addressing and exploring.

When my children have a teacher or coach who yells, I remind them to listen to what they are saying, rather than how they are saying it. If anything the coach says is helpful take it, if not leave it alone for now but try not to take his tone of voice so personally. I remind them they can use this same concept when I raise my voice. Not that I ever raise my voice. Nope. Not me.

My mother and I were clueless about the spiritual nature of the experience we were sailing through together, let alone the opportunities it presented for our development into more mature individuals. Still, everything I was going through and was yet to go through would push me toward exhaustion. The many unskillful ways I've lived throughout my life prepared me for the cracking open of my egoic shell, which would eventually allow my true being to step out of the shadow and into the daylight.

RESOURCE

Brene Brown offers a wonderful online learning community called Courageworks developed to bring her research on courage, vulnerability, shame, and empathy to a global audience. She has a wonderful program called "The Gifts of Imperfect Parenting". You can learn more at www.courageworks.com

CHAPTER 8

THE CHALLENGE OF THE TEEN YEARS

"There is a voice that doesn't use words. Listen."

- Rumi

M Y OLDEST SON recently launched into puberty and the on-slaught of hormonal and life changes it triggers. With this new phase of his life I'll have the opportunity to allow him to take flight, with my blessing instead of my fears. Instead of being constantly triggered by his teenage outbursts, eye rolls, and his perfect clarity that I just don't understand anything, I'll more often than not smile inside that he is doing just what he is meant to be doing at this stage of development. He's doing the hard work of differentiating from me and I'm doing the even harder work of not taking it personally! Because I won't take it personally, each moment of drama will likely pass quickly. I'm also learning to remember that he eats approximately eight meals a day and to budget more time for grocery shopping. Just to brag a little, I must also add that he is the most emotionally intelligent, interesting, and kind teenager I know. Not that I'm biased at all.

It's also the case that, to the degree he has already soaked up *my* fear, he too will have an opportunity to master this aspect of himself by diving into his calm, confident, competent center whenever the anxiety he picked up from me exerts its destabilizing negative energy.

It's at this point that a do-over of sort comes into play. If you have children who are a little older now, do you recall how, when they were one or two, they began to express themselves in a way that manifested an emerging awareness of their separateness from you? With their developing of motor skills, they were gaining a sense of independence.

As the journey progresses, our little ones tend to throw us a curve. They suddenly exhibit a clinging need for us—a trait that begins to dominate especially in the third and fourth years. Following the magnificent show of independence that occurs in what we commonly refer to as "the terrible twos," it's as if they have a deep need to return to the security of home base.

Hearing the mixed messages of "I don't need you" and "I need you," our goal is to respond to both in the early years and again in the teen years by combining reassurance with a gentle encouragement towards independence. Being skillful in this way is easier said than done, but certainly worth working at. If we as parents are needy, it's easy to feel rejected by our toddlers growing independence—and later the teen's.

We may react to our child's need for both reassurance and independence by making the mistake of either overly restricting or clinging. What's needed is the exact opposite. A child or teen needs serious cheering on to continue moving outward, with the reassurance we're right there with them emotionally. Can we notice when we are holding them back because we want to hold onto them?

As a child enters the teen years, this same gentle allowing of freedom, while simultaneously providing a safe, supportive, reassuring nest, is crucial. Instead of feeling either held onto or out in the cold, both of which are horribly frustrating for a young person at this stage of development, the teen then feels affirmed.

A teen's desire is to be both a separate individual *and* connected in a loving familial relationship. This kind of loving relationship and magical polarity helps our teens grow.

Peer Group Power

I mentioned earlier that after the move to Florida, I didn't feel as though I fit in with any group. When teens don't feel they belong, they don't have a solid base where they can truly be themselves without apology. Because of this, they may become a loner or find a group to join that puts them at risk.

For a growing number of our young people today, the groups to which they gravitate to completely replace the parental relationship. If strong, meaningful connection isn't available at home, friends fill the gap.

Why such a powerful attraction to their peers? And what is the concern? This is normal for teens, right? Dr. Gordon Neufeld, author of *Hold On To Your Kids: Why Parents Need To Matter More Than Peers* believes that having close friendships during the teen years is healthy and needed. However, Dr. Neufeld believes it's just as critical for the parents to be the primary attachment figure for children all the way through the teen years. When teens are overly peer oriented it undermines family cohesion and interferes with healthy development. Parents should always play a major role when their teen looks for critical guidance.

RESPECT—A KEY ELEMENT OF SUCCESSFUL PARENTING

The teen years are inevitably challenging for parents and young people alike. As they get older the awkward dance of separating and drawing close requires us to treat our teens with respect. Without respect, the dance fails.

But you might say. "The one thing I can't get my teen to do is show me respect. I've tried grounding, taking away their iPhone, shutting the computer down, turning off the TV. Nothing seems to work. They roll their eyes and talk to me in a tone that's just plain ugly."

Although it would be super lovely if our teens showed us the respect we felt like we deserved all the time, this just isn't a realistic expectation. What I'm talking about here is *how we respect our teens,* even when they are not only being disrespectful but even downright hateful. I know this sounds crazy but stay with me.

To suck it up and get curious in response to a disrespectful teen requires letting the hurt we feel roll right off us when they roll their eyes. Does this sound like letting them get away with stuff? Does it seem we're taking the easy route instead of administering what's commonly referred to as "tough love?" I don't believe so.

Instead of—for the umpteenth unsuccessful time—making an issue of something like eye-rolling or the way our teen talks to us, the way forward I have found most helpful is to tune into the *message* being conveyed through such behavior. Our teen is telling us something extremely important. The reason they are doing it in such an ugly way is that it's the only way they know how to get our attention. Can we be open to the idea that they escalate things because *we haven't been listening?*

The first step I take to amending a situation that's fractured like this is to resist raising my voice or getting angry. Not only do I not raise my voice, even if they are being unkind to me, but in that moment, I don't even correct them. When I'm growled at, I simply try to bite my tongue until the energy shifts and he can hear what I'm saying. This might be one of the most difficult things to do as a parent. What if we stopped taking our children's anger so personally? I blow it plenty of times with the whole non-reactivity thing, but we are going for good enough here!

In the silence that arises when I don't react, I'm able to listen for what the issue really is. What have I been missing? What have I been imposing from *my* agenda that they now feel a need to reject so adamantly? My job is to learn how I may have been violating their soul's purpose with my own needs or desires for things to be a certain way. He is his own person now, and I need to get out of his way while simultaneously loving him like crazy.

This does not mean I can't tell him how he makes me feel, but ideally I only share this when I'm calm and collected. Understanding and being curious about how he feels will go a long way towards maintaining connection between the two of us as he grows into adulthood.

Our Teens Need Open Communication

As a teen, I thought I knew everything and I had it all figured out. I spread my wings and pushed the limits. "Don't tell me how to do something" was my mantra. How do you suppose my mother took all this? It was not always an easy ride for the two of us. Is it ever?

> In the silence that arises when I don't react, I'm able to listen for what the issue really is. What have I been missing?

Parents I work with often think it's their "right" to tell their teens what to do and how to do it. No, I don't believe it's our right. My part is always to awaken to the fact that I've possibly failed to tune into my children so badly that they finally have become defiant. The way I see it, my teen is always serving as a mirror for me. If I have the courage to look into it, I may learn something extremely important about how I've related to them so often out of fear instead of out of trust.

Our teens have a right to learn for *themselves* and have us zip our lips, unless of course their physical safety is in harm's way. We shelve our fears and begin to trust them. If we *do* in fact manage to keep quiet when everything in us wants to tell our teen what to do, we may just find they actually ask us for our support, wisdom, or insights This is a risky moment. Such an invitation can easily become our cue to jump in with too much advice, which can destroy the connection and trust our teen is inviting. Teens need encouragement to trust their judgment, not our verdict on what they should or shouldn't be doing. I always consider myself honored to offer my support.

Upon being issued an invitation to give my opinion, the approach is always tentativeness and collaboration. This sets the stage for us exploring an issue together with deep respect for our often-incompatible viewpoints.

I've found It's one thing to discuss a situation with my teen, coaxing them to explore their own deepest feelings, and quite another to dictate the "right" thing for them to do. Insisting on my rightness accomplishes nothing except to incite them to blow off my advice—advice that, could I have delivered it in the way *they* need it, might in fact spare them a ton of pain.

Our teens need to continue feeling deep connection with us so we can be there for them when they need us as they journey towards independence. Such connection can only happen if we respect their right to privacy, so they hopefully don't feel the need to hide their life from us. Ideally, they feel they can be transparent—that they can tell us *anything*, and we won't be shocked, hurt, or reprimand them. This is a time for us to tuck our ego's vulnerability safely away, a skill not for the faint of heart.

In how many homes do you suppose teens feel they can be an open book, while also closing their door to us when they so choose, without repercussions? Answer this question and I believe you may have one answer to why we have so many troubled and lonely teens.

Our task is to rein in our reactivity, so that we maintain an accepting atmosphere in the home. To do so acknowledges our teen's right to take their own spiritual journey, which will be messy like our own, no matter how well we may have raised them. Keep in mind that messiness is the birthplace of living a mindful life and our teens will provide PLENTY of mess for us swim around in.

It's vital that we arm our teens with such a level of trust in us, including a real sense of our respect for them, that they hopefully never feel a *need* to rebel. The only reason a teen won't feel a need to rebel is that there's nothing to rebel against. That's because, as their parents, our aim isn't to control them, but to encourage and support their growing freedom. Don't you want them to leave your home at some point? Ha!

EXERCISE ON LISTENING

For the next few days listen to your teen or child without the plan or desire to respond. Just listen. Notice if, as they are speaking, you are already planning on what you are going to say next. As soon as you notice yourself do this, bring yourself mindfully back and attune with them again, listening even more deeply to whatever it is they are sharing with you. What have you been missing?

CHAPTER 9

PAIN AS A PORTAL TO CONSCIOUSNESS

"There is no coming to consciousness without pain. People will do anything, no matter how absurd, in order to avoid facing their own Soul. One does not become enlightened by imagining figures of light, but by making the darkness conscious."

– C.G. Jung

THE CONSEQUENCES OF LIVING A DISCONNECTED LIFE

During my high school surfer years, I experimented with drugs and alcohol, along with taking other unnecessary risks that led down dark alleyways dangerous for a young girl. I ended up at parties I shouldn't have been, parts of town that were unsafe, and spent time with people who did not have my best interest in mind. Pushing the edges pushed me away from feeling any emotional pain. Disconnecting from myself was my specialty.

There was a point toward the end of my college years when, even though I got good grades and worked full time, I really lost myself to drugs. I suspect I was the most highly functional screwed up person I knew.

My risky behavior was actually a way of seeking a more meaningful life. Risk didn't imply I was just being stupid or didn't value myself. Rather, risk indicated I was seeking something. It was an expression of my longing for a fulfilling life—for a life fully lived. Through all my experimenting, I seemed to be asking myself, "What else is there?"

That the answer would turn out to be *me*—the me I had lost touch with at some point while growing up—was a real surprise.

Taking wrong paths and beginning to awaken often go hand-in-hand, I've learned. We are searching, trying different things, because we're dissatisfied and therefore restless. No matter how much we try to fill the emptiness of our lives, it relentlessly gnaws at us. Becoming aware of this is how the journey to awareness often gets going. Many people I've spoken to, befriended, or coached over the years point back to the messiest or most painful time in their life as the point they became open to stepping onto the path of inner growth.

The Appeal of "Bad Boys"

Until I addressed what was really going on inside of me, my emotional stuff that was not yet integrated came out in bad behavior of some kind or another. Just like a child, I acted it out. So in addition to doing drugs, I dated the wrong kind of guys.

I was painfully attracted to bad boys. I'm talking about the kind of guys who were either emotionally unavailable, living on the edge somehow, or just a little rough and tumble.

One of my earlier boyfriends in high school, a surfer dude, hadn't a clue how to be a good partner. But does anyone in high school? Totally smitten, I worked diligently to convince him of how important our relationship should be. It wasn't long before a friend told me he had cheated on me with another girl. Despite this, I forgave him and stayed in the relationship for quite a

while longer. I really had no idea what a healthy relationship might look or feel like. I'm imagining I'm not alone in having behaved this way during my younger years.

One of my more impressive conquests was a six-foot-tall, dark and handsome unemployed womanizer. I should also mention he had major anger issues. On at least one occasion he pushed me across the room because I was upsetting him for one reason or another. Although something deep inside me told me this behavior wasn't okay, I somehow believed this was what I deserved. The drama appealed to me. It felt normal somehow. The mayhem going on inside of me was manifesting in my life.

Even after I moved away to college, this ex-boyfriend used to call me and tell me he was coming to the town where I was living. He maliciously warned me to watch my back in order to make me feel afraid of him. I was both petrified and drawn to the drama. It became "my story," which I went over and over with friends because it got me the attention I craved. Thinking back now to the girl I was, I find myself longing to sit her down, look deeply into her eyes, and remind her of her worth. She had no idea back then.

I have a nightmarish memory of being out in a bar with friends, drinking too much, and waking up about sixty miles south of where I lived. I recall opening my eyes in a strange room, with no idea how I got there or which town I was in. It turned out that a remarkably nice young man had seen me at the bar, worried about me, and drove me to his house, where he put me to bed. The next day he drove me home—talk about a blessing. That evening could have ended very differently.

On the drive home that morning, I remember thinking I was probably lucky to be alive. I also asked myself what in the hell could be wrong with me that I allowed myself to end up in such a bad situation. I felt so alone in the world, so desperate for love. Longing for a place to belong and someone to belong to, I was utterly oblivious of the need to love and belong to *myself*.

Back then I specialized in the emotionally inaccessible. "You ride a motorcycle, abuse drugs and alcohol, and push the edges in some way? Perfect. You must be for me." I thrived on the adrenaline rush and all the complication involved in these edgy relationships. This went on until I managed to fall in love with and move in with a high-functioning drug dealer—a relationship in which our happy moments were flanked by intense drama, so that I spent way too much time screaming, fighting, feeling unloved and unhappy. Did it all really need to be this dysfunctional and hard? Apparently for me that answer was yes.

Looking back, I realize these painful relationships ultimately helped lead me to my transformation. Always faithful to us, it's actually *our own deeper self* that sets us up to be drawn into just those situations that might finally get our attention. It knows what we need, and it knows how to bring it on. The question is always how much resistance will we put up before finally waking up?

It's fascinating how during that time I kept secrets even from myself. I let internal dysfunction persist for years, sort of aware that it was there but not ever really facing up to it.

When we get into real despair in our lives, we're inclined to tell ourselves that we've been abandoned somehow. In fact, the opposite is true. Whereas on the surface it may seem that life is fickle, even cruel, it's actually challenging us to awaken. The message in the messiness of it all is that the deal we've struck with life just isn't working anymore. All of these challenging experiences I had would ultimately be my saving grace. My pain would lead me back to myself, as it always does if I am willing to sit in the discomfort long enough. Had I not been so unhappy for so long I may never have had the desire to explore my inner world. I may never have stepped on the path to healing.

I tolerated a ton of pain over those years without crumbling to pieces or falling apart. Yes, I made poor decisions and put myself in harm's way, but I never again questioned my ability to work through discomfort. I'm not sure I could offer my children anything better than helping them in cultivating the ability to tolerate their own emotional discomfort.

RESOURCE

The title of this chapter is the same as a talk Dr. Shefali Tsabary gave at the Wisdom 2.0 Conference where I am an advisor. She received a double standing ovation, and I encourage you to look up her keynote and watch it. You're welcome!

Chapter 10

Life Plays Its Hand

*Life is simple. Everything happens "for" you, not to you.
Everything happens at exactly the right moment, neither
too soon, nor too late. You don't have to like it…it's just
easier if you do.*

–Byron Katie

That I needed to reinvent myself was painfully obvious,
with warning after warning showering down upon me now.
When I refused to pay attention to all the warning signs I was
being given, life took a more direct hand, as it tends to do.

I want to share with you one of the most painful incidents in
my entire life—one that took many years to find peace with.

During the period when I was doing drugs in college, I had a
dog named Lacey. My boyfriend and I were coming home from
partying late one evening and he wanted us to stay at his house. I
really wanted to bring my dog with me, but he objected. Finally,
I gave in, leaving her at my apartment in her crate.

Friends were in town and staying at my house, also partying.
They were definitely not in their right minds, which is why I was
careful to give them specific instructions to leave my dog in her
crate. "I'll be back in the morning," I told them.

When I returned the next day, my dog was gone.

I made flyers, intending to distribute throughout the neighborhood. But when I got into my car to do so, there was my lab—dead. It was the middle of summer, and she had died from the heat. When I saw her laying there I dropped to my knees and screamed. How could she have ended up in my car? Did one of my friends find my keys and use my car last night taking her with them? I'll never know.

I can't begin to describe the guilt, the sense of being entirely to blame. I had known I either shouldn't go to my boyfriends for the night or should take my dog with me, but I listened to his persuasiveness rather than to my inner voice.

The irony is that I was twenty-one at the time and volunteering at the Northern California Wildlife Rescue. I loved animals. That I had made a decision that caused my dog to die brought on a paralyzing sadness. I felt embarrassed, sick to my stomach. So ashamed of myself, I didn't even tell my future husband about what had happened to my dog until well after we married. I was sure that if he knew, he would look at me differently. Love me less. In fact, I didn't tell anyone else for many years. From an emotional point of view, I just locked it away, even though I thought about it every day well into my adulthood.

Over time, I have learned to investigate my mind without judging myself so harshly, and this was the ultimate gift towards healing. Practicing mindfulness and getting the right support helped me integrate what was causing me such stress and distress. In this way I became whole instead of split. I stopped living with one foot in life and one foot out, to avoid the pain I felt inside. I embraced each and every part of me. And so eventually I assimilated what I blamed myself for doing to my beloved dog. It would be many years later in my 40's that I would find peace with this memory through inquiry practice while attending Byron Katie's 9-Day School for the Work. Plenty needed to happen first.

DEALING WITH MY DARKNESS

It wasn't long after graduating from college but still living in my college town that I found myself taking chips of valium or xanax throughout the day. I was numbing myself to get through my two jobs and to remain in a dysfunctional relationship. I ultimately realized how depressed I had become.

Thankfully, the sensible part of me knew enough to seek therapy. I can remember walking into the therapy office for the first time to visit a little old lady to whom I would pour out my heart. Honestly, she seemed like someone who couldn't possibly be of help to me. She seemed too old, but was probably the same age I am now! Yet her guidance and wisdom put me on the path of beginning to know myself—to know what I knew but had been ignoring. Why do we do that? Ignore our inner voice?

During my time with this older wise woman I began to understand why I had gotten myself into so many bad relationships with men. "Daddy issues" is what we called it, and it was a doozy.

It quickly became obvious that I had a bone to pick with men, left over from my parents' divorce, and I was playing it out over and over again with the men I dated and even lived with. A lightbulb came on during those therapy sessions. I decided then and there that I would never remain in a dysfunctional relationship with a man again. Rather than always having a boyfriend, which I realized helped me avoid the feelings of loneliness and emptiness that haunted me day and night, I was going to be happy, find meaning, and do it all on my own. I was the one I was waiting for.

As I prepared to leave my college town and drug dealer boyfriend, I decided I wanted to move to San Francisco. Packing up my car and my cat, along with what money I had, I drove out to San Francisco to start a new life. Seriously. Just like that. Looking back now it seems so brave. At the time, all I could sense was pure clarity.

I've worked with countless clients over the years who just like me struggled to enter into their darkness and shame. Parenting is a perfect set up to teach us how to come in and out of the darkness, sometimes on a daily basis. My children have taught me like no one else how to remain in a situation or emotions that feels uncomfortable long enough to let it pass or receive its message.

> My children have taught me like no one else how to remain in a situation or emotions that feels uncomfortable long enough to let it pass or receive its message.

Reflection

Think of a difficult time in life. What did you learn from this experience? What strengths did you develop or realize you had? How did this learning impact your future self?

CHAPTER 11

DON'T AVOID THE PAIN

You are not supposed to be happy all the time. Life hurts and it's hard. Not because you're doing it wrong, but because it hurts for everybody. Don't avoid the pain. You need it. It's meant for you. Be still with it, let it come, let it go, let it leave you with the fuel you'll burn to get your work done on this earth.

— Glennon Doyle Melton

AFTER MY MOVE to the Bay area in my mid-twenties, I certainly dated, but I refused to date schmucks. I committed to not having a serious boyfriend for the first eighteen months in my new city. Yes, it sounds like an arbitrary number, and it was. But it was *my* number, and no guy would talk me out of it.

I had no hesitation in letting men know that I would happily date them, I might even spend the night with them, but not to count on getting a girlfriend out of it. As you might imagine, many of those I dated were sure I was "the one," which I'm pretty sure stemmed from the fact that they found me unavailable to them in that way. Go figure.

I confess I did manage to date one more emotionally challenged guy at this time. He was charming, handsome, and clearly unavailable. There I was being drawn to the chase all over again. Couldn't I fix him? If I cared for him enough wouldn't he come around?

I actually ended up having to push him off me one evening because he seemed to find it hard to believe that buying me an expensive dinner did not guarantee sex. I can remember the panic from that moment as I quickly assessed where I was, how much bigger he was than me, and how angry I would make him by saying no. Thankfully, I was able to storm out of his apartment, and kept myself safe. This was my last indiscretion.

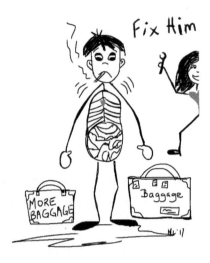

I swear this is true. No more. Not ever.

In actuality, I had finally come to a place where I would prefer to be alone than with someone who didn't adore me. I was finally comfortable being alone with myself. Who knew I was such good company?

Eventually, after all the dating, finding my own two feet, and falling completely head over heels in love with myself, I met the man I would someday marry. I had known him all along as the friend of my best friend Michael. Riccardo had a high bar to reach because I was hell bent on only dating someone exclusively who was willing to be an equal partner to me. I insisted on a man who could honor my uniqueness, appreciate me, but give me plenty of space to be my own person. We certainly had some rocky roads and still do, but ultimately, he restored my faith that mutual love and respect could exist between and man and a woman. He's still learning to stand in the fire with me without looking away, but he works to meet me where am I every day of my life. Through the Mankind project where he sits in circle each week to the Inside Circle Foundation where he's involved in deep transformational prison work, he has found an inner journey of his own. Not a moment goes by when I'm not grateful to have a life partner who is willing to do the agonizing work of looking within himself. It's an honor to share that kind of life and that kind of love. And isn't this just what our children need to see from us? They are watching closely to see if we choose to step into the fire and magnificence of self- discovery.

ADDRESSING PAIN FROM THE PAST

For those of us into avoidance there are many ways to numb our emotional pain. We either eat to excess or go after forbidden things like cookies and candies. We partake of one or two (or more) glasses of wine every evening. We busy ourselves running errands, doing chores, checking Facebook or email—anything to keep us occupied. We distract ourselves by keeping the music or television going because we're more comfortable with background noise. And the cell phone, always the cell phone. We can't possibly not respond to that "ding" when we hear it. Most of us go through life numbing our pain in these and many other ways.

When we ignore the pain life has presented us with, we risk playing it out again within our families. In fact, I would say that the best preparation we can ever do for becoming a parent is to lean into our pain.

It took many years to slap myself out of the fog I had been living in. This is a lifetime of work, and that's okay. Becoming conscious has been like a game of peekaboo for me. As a parent, one moment I'm in complete bliss, and the next I'm in the deepest, darkest dungeon of my pain. Waking up isn't easy, but it's better than repeating the same dysfunctional patterns over and over again.

The way out of emotional pain is to be *with* the pain. Dive into the pain, see it for what it is, address what it's requiring of us in terms of making some changes, and move on. Or not. Sometimes growth can be stubborn. But if we're making this effort, we can at least be sure our past doesn't become our identity. We gradually move beyond the pain instead of carrying it with us through the years. After all, how long do we want what happened to us years ago to rule and ruin our life?

If the amount of pain you are carrying is just too heavy, it may be helpful to find a counselor or therapist as I did, if that is available to you. The right person can help us tune into our pain and work with it, so that we integrate it wholly into who we are today.

Facing our pain head on, sets in motion a path of healing. Emotional energy that's been locked up trying to manage this pain can be released and become available for our everyday life. At the same time, we can begin to welcome having gone through the experience and what it has taught us.

I don't want to, in any way understate the courage it took to sit with myself in order to bring my painful memories to a point of resolution. This took real courage and support. Certain kinds of trauma absolutely require us to seek outside help. When I stop to listen to what's going on inside me, it can sound quite insane. But if I'm brave enough to be with such insanity, I find myself becoming increasingly free of the limitations it places on me, not least of which is its drain on my energy and its negative effect on my health. At some point along the way I spontaneously found myself, more often than not, noticing what's going on in and around me, and not over-reacting one way or the other. This is the game of peekaboo I just mentioned. Sometimes I'm able to be non-reactive and sometimes I'm not. But over time I slowly became what is often referred to as "conscious" or "mindful." And really, I should say that I was able to *access* consciousness or mindfulness once and awhile. The truth is we spend most of our days in a bit of a fog and can congratulate ourselves for those moments of mindful awareness. In practicing coming home to ourselves, again and again, we gain more access to these parts of ourselves. What we practice grows.

It's important to emphasize that no one escapes life's messiness altogether. I stress this because I've noticed how many advocates of mindful parenting (or mindfulness in general) make light about the realities of daily practice. The truth is, it's really hard to parent and live mindfully. It requires a great deal of energy. Some days I just want to crawl in a hole and have everyone leave me alone. Screw mindfulness and being aware today, I'm tired! This path is not for the faint of heart.

I recognize that since my efforts at parenting well can only ever be "good enough," my boys will of course have their share of issues to work through in the messiness of their own families when that time comes. We are all somewhat recovering from our childhood. This is the nature of the journey of awakening within our homes.

REFLECT

Do you have pain from your past that requires your attention? Are you willing to reflect, journal, or receive support to begin to integrate this pain into who you are today, embracing it as you learn from it?

CHAPTER 12

RETURNING TO WORK AFTER BABY

We delight in the beauty of the butterfly, but rarely admit the changes it has gone through to achieve that beauty.

— *Maya Angelou*

LUCKY FOR US, the journey towards greater awareness isn't relegated only to the home, but to all aspects of our life.

When my husband was in business school, setting the stage for the next chapter of his career, I had the privilege of staying home with our first son. Tyler had colic, which meant he woke up most nights, unable to sleep, at times screaming for hours. At the time, we were living in a one bedroom apartment so I spent many nights huddled up in our closet with Tyler to save our neighbors from the noise. As this continued into the fourth and fifth months of his life, I kept expecting to become distraught as a result of the immense disruption it brought into our lives. Even though it was a very challenging time, I surprised myself to find that all I felt was love. And exhaustion. Serious exhaustion. I realized that, for the first time, I was in a really trying space in which I didn't know what was going to happen, yet I was tapping into a fountain of resilience that amazed me. Amazing what the love of a child can awaken within us, huh?

Somehow, I managed to simply be with the situation as it was without expecting it to change. Of course, I hoped it would change at some point, but I didn't obsess over it. Rather than believe the stories in my head about how I should be concerned that something must be fatefully wrong with my son, I found myself in a state of joy. Here I was swimming in this messy soup that life had cooked up for me, feeling at peace. At this point in my life I was not involved in regular mindfulness practice, but having listened to many guided meditations over the years and having read a plethora of books, the seeds which were planted had begun to grow on their own. I often give credit to my children for nudging me on my spiritual path.

Deep within, I knew the tranquility I was experiencing wasn't of my making. Life itself had brought it about. Tyler showed up here to teach me how to be with what seemed like the impossible. That's the whole point of living mindfully in a messy world—keep treading water, remember to breathe, and keep our eyes and hearts wide open.

Not long after Tyler turned four months old, I was holding him one day when two huge realizations hit me. The first insight screamed, Holy Cow! You are the first person I know who I'm biologically connected with. I mentioned earlier that I had been adopted without ever feeling distressed about not knowing who my biological parents were. But in that moment, looking at Tyler, I found a feeling of connection that was new to me. My eyes welled up with tears and I had a sense for the first time that I was exactly where I needed to be, with no reservations. I felt I belonged in a way I hadn't before. Now, I don't want to insinuate that I didn't belong with my adoptive family because that is

not at all the case. But something about growing my own family just brought me to my knees.

The second realization I had in that moment really blew me away. It was a nice piece of synchronicity. I knew my parents didn't adopt me until I turned four months old, and previous to that time I lived with a foster family with whom I have never had contact. The question hit me like a ton of bricks, "Who in the world took care of me until I was four months old?" It seemed like a lifetime had passed, by the time Tyler grew to four months old. The sleepless nights, first smile, worries, and memories seemed endless. My mother had several letters from my foster mother prior to the time of my adoption. She shared with her that I liked to play peekaboo, liked to hold her finger while I drank my bottle, and was drawn to the color red. Up until this point, surprisingly I hadn't thought much about her. But now, holding my son at the same age that I had been adopted, I basked in a sense of wonder and gratitude for this woman who had cared for me. Who was she? Did she ever think of me?

This time of our life, living in Santa Monica, had little to no emotional drama aside from Tyler's colic and our lack of sleep. I started finding my parenting groove and enjoyed a sweet, simple life with my family, as my husband completed his MBA.

A DESPERATE MOTHER

When we returned to San Francisco, my husband began his career in commercial real estate. Once you have a child, security seems to move up the totem pole of important issues, doesn't it? If you have a little one and lose your job, you can't just move in with your best friend for a while as you could when you were single. So after a year and a half at home, it was time for me to go back to work. I didn't want to leave our son to go back to work, so I came up with the grand idea to somehow work evenings. Having been a waitress for over ten years in my twenties, I marched myself into a restaurant and was hired on the spot.

This turned out to be a terrible idea for so many reasons. I was absolutely exhausted from working late and waking up early with a toddler. What in the world had I been thinking? Torn in the way so many mothers are about needed to get back to work, I experienced desperation! I knew staying home and eating up our savings was no longer an option, something had to give.

Quite out of the blue while I was waitressing one evening, a former colleague of mine called me. The first ten years of my career in San Francisco had been working as a contract recruiter. I had taken a bit of a hiatus as a primary school teacher for a couple of years before having my first child, but had decided to leave teaching and wasn't sure what I would do next. In this phone call I found out my former colleague had taken on an executive role in a startup and needed someone to help him hire the right people. Negotiating a 10 a.m. to 4 p.m. day in the office, I went back to work as a recruiter. But what to do with my little guy during the day while at the office?

While working at the restaurant, I used to drive a young woman in her twenties home after our shift every evening. Ashley loved her work as a waitress about as much as I did, which meant basically not at all. On one of my last nights driving her home, I asked if she might be interested in being a nanny. She was always so sweet to Tyler when she visited the restaurant, and he seemed to really like her. Just like that, she agreed, and it became clear to me that I had needed to take that waitressing job to find her. Amazing how the universe sets these things up for us.

Of course, I believed I needed to be home with Tyler and Ashley for the first couple of weeks to help him transition to my absence. Surely she needed me as a bridge to helping Tyler get acclimated to being with her and how she did things. I found myself humbled the first morning Ashley showed up and Tyler, beaming a huge smile, waved his chubby little fingers and said, "Bye-bye, Mommy!" Clearly, I wasn't needed here and could go off to work. I had agonized over leaving him for no reason. This kid would be fine without me. Go figure.

We can become hypnotized by our anxiety, to the point it rules us. I was so caught up in my thoughts about how awful it would be to leave our son, and how desperately he needed me—how no one knew his routine like I did, and how he couldn't possibly be okay if I wasn't there. The situation didn't turn out at all to be what I had made of it in my mind. I was sad to be leaving Tyler, but I had been blessed to find an amazing work situation, and it all turned out to be not that big of a deal. How often we build things up in our mind quite needlessly, particularly when our insecurities and fears are involved. Now, it's not lost on me that I happened to be unbelievably lucky to have found a situation where I could work less hours in the office and finish up at home in the evening. This was an incredible privilege so many working mothers do not have. Many of us will have the opportunity to create the life we wish for around our work schedule and many of us will have a lot less flexibility. I'm sending extra love out to the parents who have to be gone all day and may even need to log on again in the evening. I experienced this later in my career and it is another whole story in balancing home life with work life.

To Help Others, First Help Yourself

After working out of the home for a little under a year as a recruiter, I decided I would only take recruiting contracts that allowed me to work from my home office. Eventually we had a second child named Brody, and I felt incredibly blessed not to miss his infancy. At this point I was making a good amount of money and calling my own shots in my independent business. To anyone from the outside looking in, you'd think I had it all, and I seemingly did. Yet I felt something calling to me from *inside* me, urging me to explore myself and my vocation more deeply.

This is where it all started going downhill for my poor husband, who up until now enjoyed a wife who was at home with his children and also bringing home the bacon. I had been thinking about what my next career move might be for some time and decided to become an executive coach. When I told my husband I wanted to become a coach and would be signing up for a year-long training, he wasn't thrilled. Giving up a good income to go back to studying felt risky to him, and I couldn't argue that it wasn't. To ease the transition, I continued contract recruiting alongside the coaching program to help us make ends meet. I now had a busy part time job, two children, and huge commitment to my yearlong coaching program. I couldn't have been happier because I was following my inner compass.

When I went away to school for the first four-day weekend of my coaching program at New Ventures West, at first I decided to come home in the evenings and reconnect with my family. Before long, I realized that transitioning in and out of the family while doing this surprisingly deep inner work was just too difficult, so I began sleeping out of the home through those weekends.

Staying away felt new, since I hadn't left the kids much, and I was torn by the idea of going away for four days at a time. There was an internal pull that said, "You shouldn't leave your kids." However, I found another, quieter voice I needed to make space for, speaking to me of my calling and purpose in the world.

In practice, I found that by not stepping back into "Mommy, Mommy, Mommy" each day of my program, I could really take time for *me*. This began a process of honoring a life for myself, quite separate from my roles in the family. The growth I experienced from being away was well worth the fears that came with it. The mother who returned at the end of each weekend was closer and closer to experiencing moments of herself as a whole person, along with an acceptance of the fact that life is messy and I could still find joy in it.

It was during this time of my life, while going through this transformational program when, I began to practice mindfulness and meditation regularly. I need to say that, as much as this time in my life enriched me, it was also a painful period. I felt unseen by my family. I tried to explain to my husband what kind of inner work I was doing, but he couldn't truly understand because he had no context for what I shared with him. When I shared stories with him he looked at me like I had two heads. I ultimately had to accept that he had no need to understand, since it wasn't his journey. The real problem I had was that *I wanted to be seen*. It was my issue, not his. And lord knows, it's not my children's job to see me.

I have to smile at another moment when it became obvious that my path of personal growth did not need to be understood by my family. After several years of day-long retreats and squeezing in practice wherever I could muster, I attended a long-awaited five days of silent retreat at Spirit Rock Meditation Center. My boys could hardly believe I intended to sit in silence for five whole days

As my children bemoaned my impending absence and asked who would take care of them I gently explained, "Need to find your baseball glove? Want a glass of milk? Trouble with your homework? Find dad. He's your guy."

During the five days, I had a profound personal experience. Upon returning home, everyone seemed happy to see me. However, after the warm greeting, the next question was, "What are we having for dinner?" Just like that, they called me back into my role as a mother. No one asked what my experience had been like. In fact, they imagined I had been to a spa relaxing for five days. No one imagined how exhausting and difficult so much of the five days had been. They didn't know how much I had fought for freedom from my own mind. Nope, I was just mom.

I'm reminded of a wonderful book by Jack Kornfield titled, *After the Ecstasy, the Laundry* which shares so eloquently that even after the ecstasy of spiritual practice we are still faced with the day-to-day tasks of our life. We are faced with the laundry.

I will admit, the thoughts that flashed through my mind upon returning was, "Seriously? You don't have dinner planned for *me* already?" Didn't they all know what grueling inner work I had been doing the last five days? The comical aspect of this is that, towards the end of the retreat, we had all been prepped for just this situation. Our families simply saw us as having been on vacation. The treasure in this was that I could laugh at myself as I realized my work to become more awake and aware just wasn't that special to the rest of the family. No one but me seemed concerned with the awakening I experienced during my five days of silence. I remained simply mommy to them, and so I went back to being mommy and integrating the work I had done while away into my day to day life.

It's About You Silly!

When I chose to change careers, and go through a coaching program, my plan included studying how to help others figure out whatever *they* needed to figure out. Sounds like a good plan, right?

Once in the program, I learned quickly that I first needed to do work on my *own* inner world with my plethora of emotional issues (still working on that plethora of issues by the way). In fact, to be a good coach I would pretty much be doing this inner work for the rest of my career. Surprise! *I* had to evolve before I could support others. This came as a bit of a shock because it wasn't in my original plan. I had no idea what I'd gotten myself into.

I'm often struck by clients and friends who anxiously tell me how their child needs to be able to manage their anxiety. I particularly hear this in the Little League baseball culture, where parents often become quite upset about their son not being able to calm down when pitching, or not being able to stay calm when batting. Yet the parents themselves are unable to stay composed while even talking about it. They themselves are super anxious! Not that I have ever been anxious about my son while he's playing sports. Who me? Ha!

It's as if mindfulness is for someone other than ourselves. People ask, "Can you teach my kids to be mindful?" Or, "My husband needs to hear this." Everyone wants everyone else to change. But during my coaching program, I learned with no uncertain terms that it's when *I* change that truly substantive change occurs. As Gandhi said, "*Be* the change you want to see in the world." I've never had a greater impact on the world around me than when I'm focusing on my own development.

It often only takes one person to stabilize others. I've noticed that when I'm grounded, peaceful, and calm, the rest of the family attunes to me even without realizing it. If I can keep myself in that calm center instead of reacting when I'm triggered, I can easily support my family in just about any situation. However, if the kids are screaming or bickering and I react strongly, I can generally count on a disaster to ensue. Now, I'm careful not to blame myself if a disaster happens, but I am willing to investigate the part I played in creating the energy that caused it.

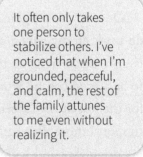

It often only takes one person to stabilize others. I've noticed that when I'm grounded, peaceful, and calm, the rest of the family attunes to me even without realizing it.

I began to find that even when family relationships were in shambles, if I could only be present, healing often occurred. A conversation would eventually follow to support the repair, but that calm connection always kick-started the reconciliation. Building the muscle of being centered and present is as difficult as any physical workout, but the benefits are no less.

CRACKING MYSELF OPEN

Cynthia Occelli who is an author and writer filled with oodles of inspiration writes, "For a seed to achieve its greatest expression, it must come completely undone. The shell cracks, its insides come out, and everything changes. To someone who doesn't understand growth, it would look like complete destruction."

Learning about myself certainly felt like complete destruction at times. I discovered I had illusions about myself even as a coach. Ironically, because I believed it was really easy for me to connect with people, that part of coaching was a breeze for me. Building trust with my clients came with ease, and this was one aspect of myself where I felt confident.

However, at one point during my program, a master coach was observing me during a coaching session, and the client I was working with just kept agreeing with me. I noticed something didn't feel quite right and asked some additional questions to go deeper in our conversation. Later, when we were downloading feedback from the experience, it came to light that my client was trying to please me because he liked me so much. This of course goes against everything one is seeking to accomplish in coaching. I wouldn't be able to support anyone if my clients just wanted to please me. The coaching relationship was about them!

While I worked with coaching clients, the safe and cozy part of me that found it easy to be liked and trusted actually worked against me at times. As the founder of the coaching program,

James Flaherty described it, my style and approach were seductive, in the sense that I could easily draw someone into my orbit. However, it undercut my effectiveness. Being liked as a coach just isn't enough. The very best coaches are able to walk a fine line between loving their clients fully while also bringing a fierce honesty to the relationship. To resolve this problem, I needed to explore why I had such a need to be liked.

This initial exploration alone took many months (and goes on until this day) and walked me into some of the deepest parts of my psyche. Stepping into the messiness won again.

I was always drawn to a sign that hung in the front of the classroom of my coaching school, that I now have on my refrigerator door. "Don't believe everything you think," it reads. It became a bit of a mantra for me. I discovered the importance of regularly questioning who I found myself to be.

This self-observation about needing to be liked led me right back to my old issues of anxiety that were so present back in college and had plagued me as an adult. Now I began to pay attention to my anxiety in a way I hadn't before. I didn't judge it as either good or bad, but simply noted, "Okay, I'm anxious right now." It was like watching myself as a third party. This had the effect of enabling me to separate myself from what I was experiencing at any given moment. "Interesting that I'm anxious right now," I would note to myself, without getting all caught up in the drama and story of why.

The coaching program took me deep into a place of healing. During some extensive inner work with my personal life coach, I revealed secrets to her from my past, such as my dog dying in college, that caused me to experience a great deal of shame. I can recall making the initial confessions to her. My coach looked at me with so much love in her eyes as she explained with a smile, "This is why you get to serve others. You've touched the darkness in yourself, and you are learning to shine light on it and grow from it. It's having gone through such experiences that gives you the honor of being able to support others." (Thank you, Annette)

This was a tipping point in my life.

As I touched the darkness of my past in a new way, there were moments when I felt I was looking down on my life, seeing myself in little pieces all over the floor. However, the breakdown led to the breakthrough.

While the breakdown did its work on me, nothing seemed to make sense. But as I sat with the confusion, the mess of my past, and the pain that resulted, pieces of who I am began to reassemble themselves into a fresh, coherent pattern. I was seeing the world through a new lens, experiencing myself and my life differently. Being supported in stepping into and out of my own darkness was a gift I could never have imagined until this moment in my life. I find this experience continues to repeat itself as I explore the many parts of who I am becoming and unbecoming. My messy mindful life had taken on a whole new meaning.

1-Minute Centering Practice

Sit in an upright dignified posture. Take a few deliberate breaths focusing on the inhale and then exhale. Allow your body to feel gravity. Notice your weight on the chair or the ground. Allow your jaw to relax. Now have your mind ask your body a question: What would it be like if there was a little more ease in my being right now?

Repeat this practice as many times as possible throughout the day or when you are feeling stressed or frazzled.

CHAPTER 13

PRACTICING MINDFULNESS AS A FAMILY

When you love someone, the best thing you can offer is your presence. How can you love if you are not there?

— Thich Nhat Hahn

SINCE HAVING CHILDREN, my focus remains on giving them my attention a good portion of the time. As parents, this is what we're called to do. But I can remember the moment prior to starting my coaching program, when my boys were about six months old and four years old. I began to ask myself, "Where has the woman I knew myself to be before having children gone? Who am I in all of this?" Between being a wife, a mom, and building my career, I realized I had completely lost touch with who I am as a human being. This surprised me, because my purpose as a parent had always been so clear. I can be enchanted with being a mother yet completely lost to myself all at the same time. What a paradox to learn to hold. This realization was beautiful, but intensely disorienting.

I mentioned earlier that I had moved away from formal religion and yet still considered myself spiritual. The truth is, I would love to have a spiritual community to call my own but I haven't found one that quite fits. The closest my family has gotten is joining the Spirit Rock Meditation Center community for their family days, but those only happen four times a year and with schedules the way they are we couldn't always make it.

My friend Mike Robbins who is an author and inspirational speaker and I have spoken in jest several times about starting our own spiritual community. But seriously, that would take a lot of time! Maybe someday (What do you think, Mike?). In the meantime, my family does its best to embrace the ordinariness of life as its spiritual practice. There are endless ways of doing this. But let me tell you, being conscious of the *little, everyday* things really makes a difference. I'm talking about things as simple as taking time to play with our pets, enjoying the flowers in the garden, spying the hummingbird, tasting a ripe tomato, and watching the popcorn pop from the machine. Imagine what it would be like to bring presence and fascination to any or all of these activities throughout the day.

Taking time to relish these ordinary things brings a unique and unexpected quality to our lives. When we take time to notice, we discover that infinite pleasure lies all around us. As we learn to appreciate the ordinary, we no longer need to continually seek the extraordinary. Life itself becomes extraordinary. This is what it means to be spiritual in my little world.

Family Rituals

I've learned that my mindfulness practices ground me in the everydayness of life, so that the sacred and the secular can be one fluid practice. Ritual helps to highlight the sacredness of even the most seemingly mundane moments.

It has been such a joy over the years to create rituals that truly tell the tale of who we are as a family. It's in these moments of often brief activity that we sink deeper into connection. Either that, or the kids totally laugh at what I'm trying to do and give me the dreaded eye roll or ignore my request all together. I'm nothing if not resilient and tenacious enough to own up to my blunders and try something new another day. I've gotten plenty up my sleeve!

> I've learned that my mindfulness practices ground me in the everydayness of life, so that the sacred and the secular can be one fluid practice. Ritual helps to highlight the sacredness of even the most seemingly mundane moments.

When we are all at the dinner table together, (which admittedly doesn't happen every night), we have a tradition of holding hands and sharing something for which we are grateful, even if it's only one word. Then we pass a hand squeeze around the table. We all learned this ritual while visiting my husband's family on the east coast. It's an opportunity to pause, sense each other's presence, express gratitude, and listen to each other. Sometimes the kids are super goofy about it and so we just have a giggle and move on. Other times we find a moment of unique family resonance and relish in that for as long as it lasts.

On weekdays, before my boys left for school we used another ritual to mark the beginning of our time away from each other. It arose out of a personal need of mine, which is often how ritual arises in my house! Isn't it just all about me after all? Kidding!

When my boys began walking to school alone together, it felt strange for me to no longer be guiding their way to arrive on campus. I found myself saddened and nostalgic for an earlier time as I watched them walk out the door and down the street without me.

It was also great not to have to get out of my pajamas if I didn't have a client meeting.

But anyway, I felt like something was missing, and I began pondering what kind of ritual we could share before they left the house. So we agreed that before they left, we would stop and hold hands. We take one breath together, then squeeze hands like we do at the dinner table. By creating a moment to reflect on our entry into another part of the day, this moment of ritual enables us to feel truly connected before we venture out into our own individual lives. Particularly on the mornings when we've had any kind of family struggle, this ritual ushers in a much-needed sweetness before saying goodbye.

I remember us taking our boys to Green Gulch Farm Zen Center in Marin County for a Sunday children's program. Some thirty children of varying ages were working excitedly on an art project in a small room. Out of the blue, one of the teachers held up a metal bowl, hitting it like a gong. All of the children fell silent, listened to the sound of the bell as it faded, then carried on with their art project. I said to myself excitedly, "I should have one of these in my kitchen."

The same day, I moved my bell from my altar upstairs down into the kitchen, placing it in the middle of the room. We made a family agreement that anyone could ring the bell at any time, but only once. When the bell rings, we all pause for a moment and take a breath until the sound dies away. It's been a nice way to build a pause into our day when needed. Our boys often surprise us with the timing of their rings!

The bell serves a surprising second purpose. Although my husband and I annoy the heck out each other at times, we don't generally get into a heated argument, and very rarely in front of the boys. They may hear us disagree at moments, but rarely do they hear us argue. One evening, my husband and I began to get into a somewhat "aggravated" discussion in the kitchen. Our youngest son, Brody, who was probably five at the time, marched into the kitchen and rang the bowl, looking us square in the face as he did. We stopped, took a breath, and let go of whatever we were becoming heated about. I realized the sound of the bell had become a way for Brody to let us know when he wasn't comfortable with how we were interacting. Though at his age he found it difficult to express his exact concern, we all understood the message of the bell. Stop. Pause. It gave him some control, and it brought us back into a state of awareness. Pure magic.

DEALING WITH DIFFICULT ISSUES WITH AWARENESS AND LOVE

The idea of family meetings is nothing new. The problem is, many family meetings either degenerate into everyone trying to make their point at once, arguing with one another, or we as parents end up playing a dictatorial role. When the "feel" is wrong, little of lasting value is accomplished.

We prefer family council meetings. My dear friend Soren Gordhamer referred me to a book titled *The Way of Council,* which I found contained all the information I needed to run an effective family council meeting. Reading those pages helped me give some thought to what I was hoping to accomplish. Meetings can be either a disaster or a wonderful way of addressing difficult issues, depending on how we understand a council meeting. And sometimes they are both a disaster and wonderful as is much of family life in my opinion.

We sit in a circle and use some kind of "talking stick," which means only the person holding the stick is permitted to talk—no interrupting. The talking stick is a way of alerting us to the need for each of us to give our full attention to whoever is speaking, shelving for the moment whether we agree or disagree with their viewpoint. It's become clear in my own family that being able to express ourselves without judgment, and to know we are heard, is crucial for a healthy life together as a family.

A council meeting may at times have a theme. On other occasions, everyone talks about issues they are struggling with. The important thing is to establish a pattern of holding these kind of meetings, or the practice will fall by the wayside. Sunday mornings are a great time for us. We found that, once we got into a rhythm of meeting, the boys began asking for a council meeting whenever they needed to share something. Such meetings are especially helpful for letting family members get to know each other better, while they also help increase a person's attention span. Children also begin to understand the family story. We cover issues such as the family's values, how we push each other's buttons, and how to negotiate for what we want.

I'm also a big fan of family meetings that are all about connection. Sometimes we do something as simple as all responding to a few questions that help each of us get to know each other better. We each respond to questions like: What quality do you like most about your best friend? If you could do anything you wanted today, what would it be? Where would you most like to travel and why? What are you most afraid of? How can you tell when you are really happy?

I'm always careful not to get stuck in the rut of family meetings always being serious and about problems. That is a sure-fire way to ruin the whole concept. We all need a little levity in our lives and family meetings need that too! Another great resource for ideas on how to have these meetings with connection and compassion is a book titled *Respectful Parents, Respectful Kids, by Sura Heart and Victoria Kindle Hodson.* It's based on the theory and practice of non-violent communication and is filled with practices to support delicious connection and understanding between family members.

Don't Forget to have Fun

Our family's rituals also include activities that are simply fun. These kinds of activities bind us together and I'm sure you already have many of your own you don't call rituals.

Kitchen dance parties are a major feature of our lives. When the mood strikes us, we put on some dance music (Michael Jackson or 90's hip hop is a family favorite) and dance like maniacs together in the kitchen. It's something we enjoy not only as a family, but also when we have friends over. Life can become so dang serious, so we find it's important to take time as a family to play. We use dance parties when everyone is stressed, and when the household has become grumpy. But above all, they are about enjoying life together. The kitchen dance ritual points beyond itself to the need to *dance through life* each and every day. Even your teens can get into this if you play music they like. Seriously, let them choose the music.

The founder of Wisdom 2.0 who I mentioned earlier Soren Gordhamer shared with me something his family sometimes played at home. I challenge you to try this sometime this week! Depending on how large your family is and how much time you have, allow each person between five and twenty minutes. Each family member gets to select an activity or game in which the rest of the family will participate. It might be hide and go seek, a family meeting, yoga, time on the trampoline, a video game, or shooting baskets. Everyone gets a turn, and everyone honors each person's decision and participates fully. When the family is in a funk, I find this ritual changes everyone's mood.

Years ago my friend Jason Stirman shared with me how he went geocaching with his kids. Geocaching is a modern-day treasure hunt that uses GPS technology on our mobile devices. You choose a geocache you want to look for, ranging from easy to difficult, and you are guided through clues to a specific GPS coordinate. Then you search for the geocache in that location. It's generally a small container of "treasure," such as bouncy balls, coins, or little kids' toys. When you find it, you take a treasure and also leave a treasure, as well as sign your name in the log provided. Then you use your phone to log it on the website. It's adventurous and gets my kids to go on long hikes looking for these things. It's super fun. You can learn about it at www.geocaching.com.

> Life can become so dang serious, so we find it's important to take time as a family to play.

Rituals can involve doing something special for individual members of the family on a regular basis. For instance, my friend Christina Harbridge had a tradition of waking up her son on Tuesday mornings by bringing breakfast to him in his room. As she does so, she makes up silly new words to a song based on a popular tune. She might sing about the French toast, apples, or whatever she happens to have prepared for him. With simple rituals like this, she makes life fun for herself and her son. This woman is the queen of making life fun and unpredictable for her son...I bow to her creativity.

It's important to inject humor and play into life, isn't it? I had the honor of helping to facilitate a family retreat program with my friend and colleague Ivy Levie down at the Esalen Center in Big Sur California. As the weekend went on we magically observed the families increase their level of play and laughter. During the closing session one of the most popular memories of their time together was playing duck duck goose, and mind you we had children as young as toddlers and as seasoned as twelve years old attending. My sense told me that although the kids loved playing the game, they especially loved seeing their parent's play, run, fall, and belly laugh. I think we can all learn something from that.

REFLECTION

What are your family rituals? Which parts of your lives could benefit from adding in ritual? How do you and your family let loose and have fun? What are some new ways you can imagine adding more play into your lives? What did you love to play as a child?

CHAPTER 14

THE PUNISHMENT TRAP

"Many people think that discipline is the essence of parenting. But that isn't parenting. Parenting is not telling your child what to do when he or she misbehaves. Parenting is providing the conditions in which a child can realize his or her full human potential."

-Dr. Gordon Neufeld

IF WE KNEW THE INTERNAL challenges a child experiences on any given day, we would be much kinder to them. We would feel compassion instead of anger at the way they sometimes behave. Shelving anger and becoming compassionate empowers us to support them in whatever they may be going through. Punishment is never an effective solution, although in the moment it always feels quite satisfying. Instead, we need to understand what's driving the behavior.

As an example, when Tyler was in third grade he told me he was practicing his math facts by playing a game on his iPad. This went on for a while, until I started to suspect he might not be playing math games.

He got caught, and my inclination was to punish him. He was also expecting it, since a month earlier he got in trouble for pulling the same trick! He got no play dates and no video games for a week. I showed him and it clearly made a lasting impact. No, not at all. Not so much. Here we were again.

When I caught him repeating his behavior, I realized punishment hadn't worked, as it often does not in my experience. Instead of exploding, awareness flooded me. I was able to breathe, pause and check in with myself regarding how I was feeling.

When we talked, I explained, "I'm sad about what just happened. While you are at school, I'm going to settle down and think about it. Then we'll talk about it when you get home so we can figure something out together, since I don't think you want to lie to me. I don't believe that's your intention."

When he arrived home from school and settled in, I asked, "What is it about video games that draws you to them?" I wasn't just looking for a quick answer. I wanted him to take some time to figure out why he found himself so intensely drawn to the video games.

Naturally, he told me they were fun. I asked him if they also helped him zone out. He agreed this was the case. They were a stress reliever for him, a way to escape. So I let him come up with a plan for iPad use that he would police himself. He spent time reflecting and writing up his ideas for us to look through together. This ended the problem for the time being anyway. Negotiating screen time in our digitally connected world requires constant attention by my husband and I, but we also remember to celebrate small victories.

In this kind of situation with Tyler, the goal was to help him build his own awareness of why something matters so much to him. Why was he willing to be sneaky to get what he wanted? What was he getting out of it? And how might he handle the situation without being sneaky? Getting to the root of the problem and helping him understand himself better is the key to resolving the issue long term.

———

Early in fourth grade, Tyler found himself becoming frustrated with the pace of his reading. "I get teased because all my friends read faster than me," he bemoaned. "What's wrong with me? I must be stupid or something."

Hearing how he felt led us to a meeting with his teachers, during which it became clear that at least one of the reasons he reads slowly is because he reads for understanding. Whereas some of his friends read super-fast but retain little of what they read beyond what's required for a test, he's meticulous about making sure he understands. His teachers and I explained that as he continued to practice reading, he would likely naturally become faster over time. But speed wasn't the priority. Right now, he needed to learn to appreciate the fact he was strong in reading comprehension, which is a struggle for a lot of kids. Not only was nothing wrong, but something was very right!

A Child's Mood

Children can be moody. My youngest is especially so. His makeup is naturally moody, so that most days he swings several times from really happy to really grumpy. As he has gotten older and better able to regulate his emotions this has improved, but it continues to be a struggle for the entire family. We don't blame Brody for his moods, but instead seek to support him in getting to know himself better.

Meeting kids where they are is crucial. When Brody was younger, I discovered that it helped him to voice what he was feeling. "You seem to be frustrated," I might say to him. Then I'd ask, "How does that feel?"

He might respond by saying something like, "I'm unhappy. I

have no friends to play with. Nothing's going right. Everything's terrible. My heart feels sad."

On my best days, I don't become frustrated but instead say to him, "Let's notice how long you feel this way" and then set a timer together. The feeling never lasts for long and he learned over time that feelings come and go. I might also ask him if he wants help to feel differently. If he says he wants help, I'll often suggest that he find a  way to move his body. This is a technique I learned about while reading Dr. Dan Siegel's book titled "The Whole Brain Child." To shift his mood, Brody would very likely suggest that he jump on my bed while I hold his hands. After a few minutes of jumping a little smile peeks out as his big emotions subside. He uses this practice to this day, although now he generally does not need my prompting and jumps on the trampoline!

Recently, Brody woke up at around 5 a.m., which triggered a grumpy day. He wasn't being nice to his brother, didn't speak kindly to me, and demanded to be allowed to play video games. I decided to try to handle this more constructively than I have at times.

Instead of my typical, "Absolutely not," I said, "Let's wait until the grumpiness passes. Why don't you go play in your room for a little while? Then let's check back with each other."

He stormed off to his room. Twenty minutes later he reappeared, asking, "Mommy, can I watch a show now?

"How are you feeling?" I asked.

He sighed as he said, "It feels so much better to be calm and happy."

Since he's an artist at heart, a practice I use with him when he's angry is to suggest he go into his room and draw his anger. I sit with him, and while he draws, he describes to me what he's drawing. This almost always brings him back into alignment and into a more peaceful place. A wonderful book we have read together over the years is called "Ahn's Anger" and really helped open up conversations about our anger, what is behind it, how we embrace it, and how we best work with it.

It's always been important to me for my children to understand that feelings come and go. Even the more encompassing emotions, such as sadness and loneliness, don't last forever. As Dr. Daniel Siegel suggests, I teach my boys to let the clouds of emotion roll by. I can't always find the patience or creativity to shift things to a better track, but I've also learned not to berate myself about it either. All we can do is show up moment by moment and do our best.

IT WORKS WITH ADULTS, TOO!

It isn't only our children we punish when they upset us. My husband and I are pretty good at punishing each other as partners as well. We may go on and on over an issue that's bothering us, or we withhold from each oth-

> It's always been important to me for my children to understand that feelings come and go. Even the more encompassing emotions, such as sadness and loneliness, don't last forever.

er. It's a childish way of being, and I know it's ineffective. There's a better way, if I can get ahead of the silly behavior before it starts. I like to try replacing anger with playfulness.

For years, my husband left his toothbrush and toothpaste on the counter, even though we had two enormous cabinets with lots of space. Seriously big cabinets! More of my mother's preference for everything in its place must have rubbed off on me than I realized, because it drove me insane to see the toothbrush and toothpaste on the counter. I tried pleading with him, begging him, and even yelling at him to put the toothbrush and toothpaste away. This shaped up to be an issue of major aggravation (for me, not him).

One day, I decided to bring a little playfulness to the situation. I left a note with his toothbrush. "Dear Riccardo," it read, "I am vampire-like, similar to your wife, Michelle. I like to sleep in the darkness. Please put me away in the cabinet. Love, Toothbrush." From then on, he started putting his toothbrush away. In other words, I had to move away from my angry, frustrated state to find a creative solution to solve *my* problem. Riccardo didn't care that the toothbrush and toothpaste were on the counter. I've since used this same ploy to get my kids to put their toothbrushes away. In fact, my note writing has been rubbing off because both of my boys leave notes around the house reminding someone to do (or not do) something quite regularly these days. It works like a charm!

We won't always find a playful solution to an issue. There will be occasions when a problem proves immovable. If the other party refuses to budge, resorting to scolding and punishing behavior only compounds the problem because it spills over into every aspect of the relationship, souring the whole experience of being together as a family. Sometimes we just have to accept a situation. Would we rather live with a toothbrush and toothpaste stowed neatly away, but in a house full of stress, or would we rather find a creative solution or let it go?

PRACTICE

I've found it helpful to notice when I'm stressed over something to stop for a moment and locate where the stress is in my body. Is it in my head, heart, gut, back, neck, face? Once I know where the stress is centered, I offer a few long exhales to that part of me, repeating them as needed until the stress eases. Some days I have to locate a lot of stress and send a lot of breath.

CHAPTER 15

WHEN I "LOSE IT"

"Stir muddy water and it will stay cloudy. Leave it alone and it will become clear. Let the stream flow and it will find its way. Stop chasing contentment and it will come to you."

– Translation from the Tao Te Ching

THERE ARE STILL TIMES when I lose it. I snap, speak in a snarky tone, and sometimes raise my voice. I harbor a lot of guilt when this happens. I probably beat myself up over this more than anything else. I think there's nothing more painful for me than growling at one of my kids, followed by the look in their eyes that shows their sadness, shock, and confusion. Seriously. Ugh.

Yet the truth is that it's hard to stay calm sometimes. I've noticed that I can be so wrapped up in my own stress or issues that I'm not able to be present for what one of my kids need from me. When this happens, I blame them for making me crazy, except that I'm the one who's responsible. I have a pretty big storyline in my head that says, "You shouldn't yell at your kids. Yelling is bad." I do my best not to let that voice shame me too much. Sometimes I raise my voice. That's the deal. I'm a work in progress. It's what I do after that matters.

After I raise my voice, I find it helpful to verbalize what might

have been going on inside me that led to the yelling. I particularly want my kids, but also my husband, to know what was happening within me. After everyone has calmed down, I sit down with them, and we each describe what was going on for us. "Here's how I was feeling when I yelled," I explain. "I was tired, and I was thinking of all the things I have to do for work. You were complaining about not wanting your dinner. Mommy felt a lot of big emotions, and I'm sorry I yelled. I don't like it when I yell." I'll then usually describe ways I can intercept my yelling, like walking away and taking a few breaths or going outside. Getting some space from my stress almost always gives me a better perspective on things. I get the chance to be with my emotions and understand them better.

I've found that my boys always appreciate it when I talk through what's going on inside me. It's also a way to teach them to be aware of their own internal state. When I let them in on what I'm struggling with emotionally, they know they aren't alone when they also experience the same emotions.

I think of a time when Tyler expressed a ton of anger at his younger brother, Brody. I had been doing Byron Katie's inquiry process for some time and had also been sharing it with Tyler, who was very much onboard to using it together. On this particular occasion, I wasn't in the best state of mind because they had been fighting for some time and I had let myself spin. Tyler demanded we go upstairs and do "The Work" together right now. He said it in a voice that oozed wisdom, determination, and desperation, all at the same time!

We went upstairs with Byron Katie's special kids' worksheet and Tyler did his best to fill it out on his own but really struggled with it because he was so angry. Finally, Tyler said, "It's just not going to work this time, Mom." He seemed to be right. Although talking through the issue had enabled him to calm down a bit, we were not able to continue because he wasn't in the right state of mind in that moment. I let him know that he should be proud of himself for thinking of a way on his own to understand himself better and I assured him that what he had already done was more than enough for now.

When I reflected on what had transpired, I realized two things. First, I wasn't personally centered enough to support him in his own inquiry. I was still really triggered from all the bickering. Second, he had become so clever in doing this work that he was already seeing into the future as to what he needed to do to help bring about a solution. The solution would require him to get off his soap-box of being angry at his brother and he was not ready.

I shared this with him. "Next time we try to do this work together," I said, "I should be very calm first." He agreed. I also told him I was immensely proud of him because, despite the fact that he wasn't able to work through it all right then, he was seeing his part in his struggle with his brother even before we had completed the worksheet together. Well done Tyler.

SILENCING THE VOICE OF THE INNER CRITIC

One particular day, Tyler had several difficult things happening one after the other. He was ready to pop. His little league team had lost most of their baseball games that season and he continued to endure struggles at school with kids who were being mean to him during recess.

We were at a friend's house where Tyler was having fun playing basketball with friends, but needed to leave to go to a doctor's appointment. As parents often do, I had given him several warnings that we had to leave. Finally, I said in a more stern voice, "We have to leave *now*." Well, he freaked out and started screaming. Rather than going directly to the doctor I brought him home. It was one of the worst temper tantrums he had ever had. He was nine at the time. I told him, "I want to talk to you and help you, but I can't do that until you calm down at least a little bit." He was super muddy from playing with his friends and decided to take a hot shower to settle down. After he calmed down, he realized how bad of a meltdown he had experienced and started apologizing for all the mean things he had said to me.

It wasn't long before he began criticizing himself in a pretty intense way. I immediately responded, "No, don't be down on yourself. In fact, this is really interesting. I'm excited that you were this upset. Whenever a person is this mad, there's something important to be learned. So let's see what's going on underneath all of your emotions. Tell me, what was happening right before you got so angry?"

They had been playing basketball, and he explained, "When you pulled me away from the game, I had already lost two rounds but I was about to win." We were able to have a rich conversation about how the desire to win is a wonderful trait he possesses that enables him to be a great competitor, while at the same time it's an aspect of his personality that can get him into trouble. Sometimes he wants to win so badly that he can be mean to people he loves. "This desire to win is just something to notice," I explained. Ever since that day, he's had a gentle curiosity about his relationship to winning that has periodically come up and we have been able to talk through.

Now, the truth is, I'm a person who can easily go into a crazy mother rant when a temper tantrum starts. I could just as easily have said, "This is ridiculous. Get it together. It's just a game." But when this is my reaction, no learning takes place for me or my children. It takes true presence to find a centered state when a child is stressed and experiencing heavy emotion. These situations also require curiosity on the parent's part. Curiosity kills stress and anxiety every time. Sometimes I try to think of myself as a private investigator who needs to gather information and evidence in order to figure out what is really going on with one of my kids.

When one of my children aren't getting what they want and starts to lose it, there are only two ways forward. I either match their emotion, getting into a tit-for-tat with them, or stay present in myself and work as their ally. The key is always my ability to stay self-aware in a moment of stress. As I mentioned, I try as hard as I can (while concurrently wanting to hide in my closet) to let my mind be curious: "How interesting. Let's figure it out." This honors my child, instead of steamrolling over them by telling them not to feel what they are in fact feeling—an approach taken by so many parents I've worked with and that I've often taken myself. Steamrolling never works. Oh OK, we may get what we want in the moment, but nothing has really changed and we will be dealing with this same situation again before too long.

At my sons' school, the third-grade teachers often handle interpersonal conflict by having the kids answer three questions. For instance, if a child says something hurtful to another student, they are asked to consider, "Is it kind? Is it true? Is it necessary?" Ideally, they want the children to ask *themselves* these questions before they say anything to another child. I keep these three questions written on a chalkboard in my living room to help remind us all to use them before we are about to say something we might later regret.

> Curiosity dissolves anger and anxiety every time.

Of course, it's always ideal when we don't lose it at all, isn't it? Staying peaceful and calm in the midst of an emotional storm is not easy, but it sure does help. And for those times that we lose it or say something we wish we would not have, recovery is so important. Being able to say, "I'm sorry," and the willingness to talk through the emotions that were erupting in everyone involved. In this way, we learn and grow together.

A writer by the name of Courtney A. Walsh gets this. She penned a poem that, for me, sums up the challenge of parenting and being human. You can find it at courtneyawalsh.com. It reads:

"Dear Human: You've got it all wrong.
You didn't come here to master unconditional love.
That is where you came from and where you'll return.
You came here to learn personal love.
Universal love. Messy love. Sweaty love.

Crazy love. Broken love. Whole love.

Infused with divinity. Lived through the grace of stumbling.

Demonstrated through the beauty of… messing up. Often.

You didn't come here to be perfect. You already are.

You came here to be gorgeously human. Flawed and fabulous.

And then to rise again into remembering.

But unconditional love? Stop telling that story.

Love, in truth, doesn't need ANY other adjectives.

It doesn't require modifiers.

It doesn't require the condition of perfection.

It only asks that you show up. And do your best.

That you stay present and feel fully.

That you shine and fly and laugh and cry

and hurt and heal and fall and get back up

and play and work and live and die as YOU.

It's enough. It's Plenty."

RESOURCE:

I have studied with Byron Katie for many years. You can learn more about her process of inquiry at www.thework.com. She offers tons free videos and resources as well as wonderful retreats. If you can ever attend her 9-day school for the work consider yourself blessed. Don't let the cost scare you because she offers many scholarships. Man, oh man did I make peace with my mind over those nine days.

CHAPTER 16

GROWING MINDFULNESS

"To experience peace does not mean that your life is always blissful. It means that you are capable of tapping into a blissful state of mind amidst the normal chaos of a hectic life."

-Jill Bolte Taylor

W E'VE ALL HEARD stories of monks going off into caves, monasteries, and mountaintops to live for years at a time. But is this particular way of life in some way superior to living in a family? I think it's just different…not better or worse. Not that I wouldn't like to haul myself up to a monastery on a hill sometime.

Even if we are privileged enough to go away on retreat and sit in silence from time to time, as I have been, we come back to a family still firing on all cylinders. I learned this the hard way upon returning from an extended retreat and expected everyone to revel in my commitment and hard work. Instead, the first words I heard were "Oh Hi Mom, can you call so and so's mom to set up a play date?" I may have been in deep contemplative practice the past week, but upon coming home everything was clearly the same. While retreats can be enormously valuable, they aren't the only way to cultivate the qualities we desire. All of what we seek can be found in everyday life and within any kind of practice, be it yoga, a hike, meditation, feeling the water on our hands as we wash the dishes, or simply stepping away to take a few breaths. Our family members await us each time we return from our sacred practice (sometimes it feels like they are stalking us, but whatever).

Life has hammered home to me that it's in what happens when we return to the family, with all its chaos and demands, where mindfulness has the opportunity to be strengthened.

Everyday life in a family is fundamentally different from our mental concepts of what *should* happen on the mindful path. However, it's when we finally embrace the idea that the entire context of our life exists to support our personal growth that we see real change. To this end, life has all kinds of ways to catch us off guard, inviting us to grow in situations that arise incessantly until we face up to what they are asking us to look at.

Jon Kabat Zinn shares, "Let everything become your teacher: your body, your attitudes, your mind, your pain, your joy, other people, your mistakes, your failures, your successes, nature—in short, all your moments. If you are cultivating mindfulness in your life, there is not one thing that you do or experience that cannot teach you about yourself by mirroring back to you the reflections of your own mind and body."

The insight that life itself is where mindfulness ripens is an insight also shared by Jack Kornfield. "Your life provides the perfect conditions for awakening freedom and compassion," he writes in *Bringing Home the Dharma: Awakening Right Where You Are.* "Enlightenment and liberation are not found in the Himalayas, nor in some ancient monasteries. They are only found where you are."

It took me a while to really "get" that my family is core to my practice of mindfulness, but over time I began to see my family members, especially my children, as my greatest teachers.

Today I understand that every stressful situation in our lives, every difficult person, every challenge—it's all for us. But, so too is every joy, every success. It's all there for our enjoyment, curiosity, and learning. The trick is to be able to recognize when the stressful moments are coming or are upon us, so that we

can learn to recognize the reactivity in us and *respond* rather than *react*. Responding is constructive, whereas reacting is generally destructive. Responding requires an openness, a willingness to incorporate whatever may be true of the other's viewpoint even if we initially don't like it.

So nowadays, when my children say, "You're not being fair," in a situation in which I believe I am being fair, I've learned to try and not react by defending myself. I've discovered that as soon as I begin to defend myself, I'm creating conflict, and potentially starting more drama than is needed. I'm willing to consider the possibility that perhaps I'm not being fair and look more closely at my reaction. The reality is that they are experiencing me as unfair, and that should be enough to stop me in my tracks to at least get curious as to why. I may also stop and reflect on other areas in my life in which it's possible I'm not being fair. Could anything they are

> Today I understand that every stressful situation in our lives, every difficult person, every challenge—it's all for us. But, so too is every joy, every success. It's all there for our enjoyment, curiosity, and learning.

saying be true? Maybe. What part may I be playing in the drama that has taken over this moment? It's worth the exploration and personally tends to bring me to a more peaceful state of mind.

PRACTICE

The next time one of your children accuses you of something see if you can notice that sense of defensiveness come up. Now stop and investigate. Is anything they are saying true? Has it been true in other moments of your life? Maybe yes. Maybe no. Can you see things from their perspective for even just a moment? And from this place how are you drawn to respond?

CHAPTER 17

GIFTING CHILDREN WITH OUR PRESENCE

*Always say "yes" to the present moment. What could be
more futile, more insane, than to create inner resistance
to what already is? What could be more insane than to
oppose life itself, which is now and always now? Surrender to what is. Say "yes" to life- and see how life suddenly
starts working for you rather than against you."*

— Eckhart Tolle

O NE DAY WHEN I WAS getting a manicure and pedicure, sitting across from me was a mother with an adorable little
girl. The little girl's finger nails had just been painted, and she was
desperately trying in very sweet ways to get her mom's attention.
I found it difficult to watch the mother's obliviousness. My heart
was aching for this little girl. The woman barely lifted her head up
from her phone as she nodded and said, "Uh huh, uh huh" then
went right back to her phone.

Why did this incident bother me so much? Because I could see
myself in it. I wondered how many times I had done the same kind
of thing when one of my children needed or desired my attention.
I can tell you I'm glad I did not have babies when smart phones
had already become ubiquitous. I can only imagine the studies on

attachment that will be done on the effects on newborns, infants and toddlers from mothers distracted by technology, but that is a whole other book for someone else to research and write.

During the time of that manicure episode I had been studying with a teacher on the topic of deep listening. For me, good listening and practicing presence go hand-in-hand. The focus was on allowing someone to really be heard. I was in the kitchen cooking one evening, and my son Brody who was about five years old at the time was trying to get me to listen to something he wanted to share. I kept saying, "Uh huh," kind of paying attention but not really. You know how we do that? When he kept coming at me again and again trying to share what he wanted to say, I began feeling annoyed and this became my alarm system to pay closer attention. As my annoyance increased and I gave a little space for curiosity, I realized that I hadn't given him my real attention. I wasn't listening, and he was less than satisfied with my lame responses.

I stopped what I was doing in the kitchen, got down to his level, looked into his eyes, and listened as he shared with me what he needed to say about the tower that he built in his room and what superhero lived there. When he had been met and heard, off he went happy as pie. All that was needed was a few moments of my true presence. What a huge lesson for me.

How often do we only give our loved ones a sliver of our attention, which simply isn't fulfilling for them? If we can learn to stop and really be with them for a moment, hearing what they are trying to tell us, it takes not only less time but also less energy. And the other person isn't suspended in a dance of hopelessly trying to get our attention. All they need is for us to attend to them deep-

ly for a moment. Try it next time your child is talking to you and you catch yourself looking down at your phone nodding your head saying "uh huh". Sound the alarm!

THE FOLLY OF WAITING FOR SOMETHING TO HAPPEN

There's a scene in the Dr. Seuss book *Oh, the Places You'll Go* in which everyone is just waiting around for something to happen. It's kind of a pathetic scene where you see people just waiting in line, staring off into space, looking at the clock. I often think of this scene as I reflect on how our culture has gotten addicted to our technology. Are we not all waiting for something to happen as we stare down at the news, email, or social media?

We've all been around people who feel like life is happening to them and they have no control. We've also been in situations in which everyone is waiting for the next thing to happen and somehow distracting themselves until it does. And, too, no doubt we've all caught ourselves waiting for something, anything, to happen because we are bored out of our minds.

The fact is, many of us have real difficulty just being where we are, looking around, smelling the scents in the air, listening to the sounds of nature or the world going by—in other words, experiencing life *as it unfolds*, moment by moment.

When nothing appears to be "happening," many of us are compelled to reach for our technology. I've actually made a practice of noticing when someone picks up their phone, which always triggers in me a desire to pick up my phone. It's visceral, as if we can't tolerate the "now" in which we tell ourselves nothing is happening. Finding new email in our inbox literally releases a "happy" chemical in our brains called dopamine that causes us to seek out new email over and over again to get the next "happy" hit. The same chemicals in our brain that light up for addicts lights up for us around getting new email.

Whenever I feel the urge to pick up my phone, I bring awareness to this urge. What's driving it? Is it boredom? Loneliness? Sadness? Then I sit with whatever's there until it dissolves. And yes, sometimes I just check my email or social media sites…but learning to sit with the urge is ultimately more gratifying and keeps me away from technology addiction.

I've found it helpful to make an agreement with the family to refrain from using technology in the common area of our home. When we are in this space, we give our family the gift of our attention.

It can also be helpful to choose a day over the weekend when the whole family puts technology aside. My husband and I do all of us a big favor when we stay off technology in the evenings until our boys have gone to sleep.

A PATH TO PRESENCE

I've learned that the root of the feeling that "nothing is happening" is that I *can't be with myself*. It's a lack of the ability to be with myself that prevents me from being truly present with others. I know if I want to become more present for others, then I need to continue learning how to be present with *myself*. *Peri-*

od. Easier said than done though. Often, I don't even know I have a problem with this because being distracted is such a habit!

Because there are often hidden layers of pain within us, at first sitting with ourselves can often be unbearable. Recall how I talked about when I first had to sit in silence for twenty minutes, and I thought I was going to leap out of my skin. Yet now, I relish retreats in which we sit in total silence for an extended period of time. That's because, once I moved beneath the layers of pain and learned to be with my anxiety, the anxiety didn't have quite such a hold on me anymore. I certainly still have anxiety. Plenty of it. I just don't take it so seriously anymore.

I had to smile when, upon me return from a silent retreat, my older son asked, "Did you really not talk for five days?"

"Very little," I explained.

His response? "That's so boring."

In reality, to gift ourselves the time to be profoundly in touch with who we are under all the busyness isn't at all boring. On the contrary, it's one of the most alive experiences I have ever had, for it's what has given so much more meaning to everything else in my life.

DEEPENING MEDITATION PRACTICE

The value of meditation is that it introduces us to our inner reality. The real reality...not the one we are willing to share with everyone else or pretend to be on social media. All the heinous hard stuff once investigated becomes less scary. Sometimes things we uncover in our minds are so scary we should bring them to a professional therapist, but generally it's just general unease that rises to the surface.

To accomplish connecting to our inner reality, we must first go through the layers of pain that block awareness of this deeper self. Meditation practice first trains us to have the courage to dive into our pain, strengthening us with a willingness to just be with it. When I say "be with it," I mean neither venting the pain nor wallowing in it, but simply *allowing it to be,* observing it with loving curiosity. While I was on retreat with Jon Kabat-Zinn he once talked about the concept of "letting go" in our practice. He gently suggested we get over that phrase and instead "let it be". This simple suggestion helped to transform my practice. Letting go is a lot harder than letting something be.

An important aspect of meditation is that we don't try to stop ourselves from thinking. Early on in my practice I remember having the idea that I was supposed to block all thoughts during meditation. People tell me all the time, "I can't meditate because I can't stop my thoughts." As it turns out this is all mixed up. In actuality, the moment we notice we are having a thought during our meditation practice is the exact moment we are doing it right! Once we notice we are thinking we can choose to stay with the thought or consider coming back to focusing on the breath or another point of concentration. That is the practice!

The point isn't to try to stop our thoughts, but to practice becoming *aware* of them. Suppressing thoughts isn't helpful. Without our desire or assistance, they will appear and then pass. Some of them will be helpful and some will be hurtful. Some will be so bizarre and out of context that they make no sense at

> The point isn't to try to stop our thoughts, but to practice becoming *aware* of them. Suppressing thoughts isn't helpful. Without our desire or assistance, they will appear and then pass.

all. I've learned to appreciate each one for passing through. As my teacher Byron Katie says about our thoughts, "Thank them for sharing their life with you."

Gradually, I learned to just observe whatever thoughts and emotions were passing through me without becoming caught up in them. I came to see that my thoughts and emotional reactions weren't *me*. Thoughts are just thoughts, and emotions are just emotions, and they come to all of us in random and surprising ways we have no control over. The key for me was not to take them personally. Logical, illogical, nightmarish, even insane—it doesn't matter what passes through my head. That's all it's doing, passing through—unless I allow myself to *identify* with the stories I tell myself. And a reminder that I'm not talking about my major life trauma here, but the everyday nagging voice in my head.

This is especially helpful dealing with a stressful job. When I was working at Twitter, at times I became caught up in whatever stress might be going on around me. I found that using short centering practices to slow me down were extremely helpful to get through the day. They enabled me to be a little island of calm in the middle of a corporate storm.

I often heard from employees at Twitter that I had a stabilizing effect on them when things were really going haywire. Without my meditation and mindfulness practices, I may have struggled to stay grounded. A big part of my role was to support leaders and human resource initiatives through difficult times. I would have been of little use during those stressful times if I was a mess too. Twitter was a great place to work, a privilege; and yet things moved at a full throttle pace day after day. I couldn't have been of service in a helpful way without the ability to stay centered.

By practicing the ability to stay centered during difficult times while also just being willing to sit with my stress and anxiety, I learned that even in the midst of my messy, complicated life, I have access to a quiet, peaceful inner state. It's always waiting for me.

RESOURCE

The Center for Non-Violent Communication offers all kinds of in-person and online programs to support you in becoming more self-aware and emotionally intelligent. Some programs offered are created specifically for parents. I went through their yearlong parent peer leadership program and it was a wonderful resource to help me become friendlier with my own mind. https://www.cnvc.org/

CHAPTER 18

WHO AM I AND
WHAT DO I NEED?

"Let go of who you think you are supposed to be, and be who you are."

- Brene Brown

THERE'S ANOTHER WAY in which my children invite me to become more of who I am. I can remember getting so caught up in doing the "mommy" thing that it became my whole life, demanding all of my time and attention. At times when I have completely immersed myself in this role without coming up for air, I have found myself drowning in it.

As a mother, I've found myself gasping for air at times—and I suspect many mothers and fathers experience this but don't like to admit it. We feel guilty for being so overwhelmed with parenthood. It's crucial we pay attention to this feeling and see what it's asking of us.

I explained earlier how, while I was still single, I began noticing signs, pointers, to a deeper kind of life than I was living. I began to understand that I wasn't just a product of my genes and my environment, but that I have a deeper dimension that's the essence of who I am. Only when I at last paid attention to this inner aspect of myself did I really start to find my way to a fulfilling life.

When we give ourselves over to a mommy or daddy identity, we may begin to see similar pointers to the deeper dimension of our being that longs to be acknowledged. It may be that we start to experience a certain kind of emptiness, a sense of loss, or at times even a feeling of distress. It begins with twinges, a hunch that something is amiss. Eventually it may develop into a nagging sense that a dimension of who we are is seriously missing in our life as we're presently living it. This is not a time to feel guilty and wonder if we are a bad parent for having these thoughts and feelings. This is a time to listen deeply to what our deeper self is trying to tell us.

There came a point when I had to admit to myself that not only did my children have needs, but I had them too. Much to my surprise, after focusing so intently on my children for so long I remembered I was a person in my own right. I needed to honor myself as a woman, with an identity and a journey to be pursued completely separate from serving as the mother to two children.

It was as I increasingly became real with myself, facing up to the desires of my own journey, that I found the courage to become honest with my family about my need to pursue *my* own path as they each pursued *their* own paths. I didn't have to sacrifice myself for everyone else. At least not all the time!

Another aspect of this is that, if we ignore our deeper being as it repeatedly calls to us, choosing instead to live our life through our children, we do our children a great disservice. Ignoring our own need for a purposeful life, we place a huge burden on our kiddos. They now have to shoulder the responsibility of making us feel fulfilled. Carl Jung once said, "Nothing has a stronger influence psychologically on their environment and especially on their children than the unlived life of the parent." Just take that in for a moment.

Consequently, they may start living to please us instead of pleasing themselves—or they may rebel. In both cases, they betray their true being. No child can thrive when our hopes and dreams, and our need for acknowledgment, are all caught up completely in their lives rather than our own. Saddled with the need to make us happy, they are no longer free to be true to themselves.

To Care Is to Honor Our Individuality

Truly *caring* for our children means encouraging them to grow up true to who *they* are, not who *we* think they ought to be. Both at home, as they grow and explore their interests, and later in their work life, to be who they really are is the key to fulfillment. There's no joy to be had from betraying themselves to satisfy an image they think they need to live up to in order to make us happy. I'm always just a little bit surprised (okay, horrified) to see the eight-year-old wearing the Ivy League sweatshirt announcing that they will be attending Princeton or Stanford. No pressure there to be what their parents expect of them. Yikes.

Members of a family aren't meant to conform to one another. We aren't meant to match each other's hopes and dreams. Rather, we are here to support each other on our individual journeys, encouraging and cheering each other on.

I've coached many a woman who has been a stay-at-home mom practically all their adult lives and feel they have little to contribute to the world of work, since it's a world in which they haven't been involved. Or if they once did, it was a long time ago.

I argue that, on the contrary, if a mother has developed her own authentic self while parenting, she's exactly the kind of material you want in the workplace. Her authenticity—her ability to be true to herself despite all the demands and pressures from others—is exactly what's needed in leadership, as is her ability to negotiate calmly and fairly in the most charged situations.

I've worked with many tense mothers who are stressed out trying to fulfill their roles both at home and in their career. Step one is always to stop feeling apologetic for being a person with your own needs. Remember, put on your own oxygen mask first!

We are just as important as our children. Indeed, unless we recognize this and honor it, we are unlikely to be able to show our children their own importance.

Love Yourself for What You Love

Do you realize how hard it can be as parents to say "yes" to ourselves when it comes to honoring our personal desires and preferences?

I want to take you back to a time when I was preparing for a silent retreat. When I signed up for this retreat, I felt I was finally joining that exclusive club of individuals who have made space in their lives for deeper spiritual practice. Regardless of how dedicated I had been to my practice up until then, a part of me believed

I wasn't the real deal until I suffered in silence for an extensive period of time like everyone else. Or so I believed.

In the days leading up to my departure, an array of concerns flooded my thoughts. Would my body ache from sitting for so long? Would old emotions surface so strongly that I would be overcome by them? Would five whole days seem eternally long, or would the time fly? How much would I miss my family?

I whispered thoughts to the universe such as, "Please let my plants and flowers survive my absence. And make sure my husband feeds the dogs."

Despite my plethora of concerns, nothing prepared me for how I would feel when I read these words: "This is a fragrance-free retreat. Please do not bring any products with any sort of scent." What? No products with scent? Do these people have any idea how much I adore my day cream with cucumber and my ever-so-rich and luxurious night cream? Does this mean I also have to leave my rose cheek stain at home? And what about the special shampoo and conditioner I use because they contain no sulphates?

For crying out loud, where was I going to find the time to discover fragrance free products that suited me in such a short time? I know. I know. Pathetic.

Getting Clear About Ego

I do realize how thoroughly "first world" my concern about this fragrance issue sounds. It's totally embarrassing to admit all of this. So why couldn't I stop thinking about what it would be like not to have my beloved products with me?

When the part of me that observes my thinking finally caught up with my thoughts on this issue, I felt ashamed of myself. After all the mindfulness practice over the years, did I truly believe that to be without my products was to suffer?

Well, in a way, yes. I *was* suffering. The suffering was coming from all the things I was telling myself and believing, hook line and sinker. But then, hadn't one of my reasons for signing up for a silent retreat been to suffer at least a little bit? No way sitting in silence for five days was going to be easy. I just didn't expect it to get underway quite so soon. I hadn't even stepped foot in the retreat center for crying out loud!

A different issue concerned me even more than the fragrance-free dilemma: Who would my roommate be? I'm a light sleeper. What if she snored? Now that would be *real* suffering.

I mentioned my dilemma to a dear friend and to the teacher who was to lead the retreat. Their reactions all but mirrored each other. The look on their faces and tone of their voices was one of pure curiosity since this was a part of me they hadn't seen before.

Sharing my dilemma in this way helped me recognize the humor in my worries and enabled me to hold my concerns lightly. After all, the essence of who I am doesn't include *any* products, fragrance-free or otherwise. I could manage without them for five days.

I did end up perusing the aisles of Whole Foods for fragrance-free gems. I also spent time reflecting on what it would be like to sit in silence long enough for a bit more of my ego to unravel—though I decided to observe it lovingly, free of the customary little-shop-of-thought horrors I so often brought onto myself. After all, there's no point beating myself up over an issue I think I "should" see differently, when I really don't.

Something became clear to me through this experience. Enjoying creature comforts *isn't ego* if we are not overly attached to them. They are something to be treasured... but kept in perspective. Finding healthy attachments to our "things' and "privileges" sets up the possibility of passing this on to our children. In our media obsessed world they are sure to be bombarded with images of what they should have and how their lives should be.

To feel superior about our first world pleasures, as if we somehow deserve them more than others, *is* ego. To feel like we've "earned" them can also be ego if we don't acknowledge how indebted we are to everyone and everything that led to our being able to perform the work that enables us to enjoy them. Whether we're talking about the pioneers who carved out our heritage, the genes we inherited, the influence of our parents, the privilege of education, or countless other circumstances that have equipped us to do well in the world, we owe a great deal to so many.

But just as feeling privileged and not realizing the extent to which grace has played a role in my blessed condition is ego, so too can *glorying in suffering* be ego. Even priding myself that I sat in silence for five days can be a mark of ego. One of my favorite books that explores these topics is called *Cutting Through Spiritual Materialism,* by Chogyam Trungpa. It's a slippery slope getting caught up in the idea of being a good meditator or believing that you are more spiritual than the next guy.

LEARNING TO HONOR MY PREFERENCES

Much is said in spiritual circles about how desire produces suffering. But I suspect it isn't our natural desires that are at fault. It's *craving* that's the issue. To crave something, to lust after it, to covet it, and to tell ourselves we can't be happy without it, is entirely different from wanting to enjoy ourselves.

Far from being a mark of enjoyment, craving is a display of inner emptiness. When we feel empty inside we often try to fill the void with external things—a chocolate cake, a particular car or house, designer clothes we imagine will make us "someone". None of these are wrong in themselves. It's the *neediness* that drives us to crave them that's the problem.

Desire is quite different from craving things out of neediness if it flows from the heart. It's a sense of our worth, our value, our greatness, which causes us to want to expand out into the world creatively. We long to be the fullness we really are.

Perhaps each human soul is a divine fullness seeking expression in material form. What if the entire universe has arisen from this fullness, becoming ever more expansive, ever more complex, ever more evolved, ever more beautiful. I like to think this is the way our lives are meant to be.

What if we desire not because we are empty, but because we are full? Our heart is bursting with a longing to be with what and who we are in our purest essence. This is what I believe drives my desire for spiritual growth and pulls me towards living a mindful life. Once we awaken to our solid center and this inner fullness, there can never be the kind of emptiness that's behind the craving, the grasping, the greed, the one-upmanship, or the conflict that mars so much of our world.

THE ART OF SELF CARE

"I've come to believe that caring for myself is not self-indulgent. Caring for myself is an act of survival."

– Audre Lorde

As my friend, Suzi Lula so eloquently shares in chapter three of her book, *The Motherhood Evolution*, "self-care, or inner-care" as she calls it, "is the practice of nurturing ourselves on the physical, mental, emotional, and spiritual levels in order that we may experience an ecstatic sense of well-being, vitality, and fulfillment. It is the bridge to living an expansive, enlightened life, especially where our children are concerned."

In my corporate work with parents I've found that as a community we are often the absolute worst at finding time to take care of ourselves. We give so much time and energy to our careers and families, then find ourselves completely spent. Here's the deal. One of the most important things we can do is to care for ourselves. Period. End of story. Got it?

The older I get the more I have surrendered to the fact that I need to sleep, exercise, eat well, drink plenty of water, and weave in time for slowing down each day. If I slack on any of these items, it will not be long before my body and mind remind me so. One of the greatest gifts we can give to our children is to take care of ourselves.

Anyone else run ragged and then blame the people we love the most for feeling so cruddy? I mean, we are doing all of this for THEM after all. Don't they get it? No, they don't, because it is not their job to take care of our body mind and spirit. It's imperative that we make ourselves a priority because if we don't, no one else will. I titled this section the ART of self-care because it truly is an art. Each person has different needs and will need to make different choices. I have a friend who needs to get outside every day for a walk, and although I like to walk every day, if I don't do it I won't feel grumpy or worn down. However, if I don't drink enough water and sit in at least a little stillness, I can be a serious bear. Find what works for you and then stick to it. Now go and take care of yourself.

> One of the greatest gifts we can give to our children is to take care of ourselves

PRACTICE

Make a list of things that support your own personal brand of self-care. How much sleep do you need? Which activities and people give you energy? Which foods make you feel alive and healthy? Which people or activities drain your energy? Where can you go to revitalize yourself?

CHAPTER 19

JUST SAY NO

"When you say yes to others, make sure you are not say-ing no to yourself."

- Paulo Coelho

N OW THAT WE HAVE explored the importance of meeting our needs for ourselves, I want to discuss another key aspect of honoring ourselves and the unique journey we have chosen to take—a journey *only* we can take, and that no one can ever appreciate in the way we do.

I've been privileged to have somewhat high profile positions over my career. Because of the many connections these opportunities have provided me with, I could easily spend ten hours a week on phone calls and meeting with people who want some sort of support from me, and the truth is I really enjoy helping and guiding others. If I could pay my bills by taking all of these requests I totally would. I also know that I'm a "yes" person by nature, who seeks to please people and wants others to like me. I've had to learn to say "no." This was no easy task. And even when I got good at saying no, I often felt uncomfortable inside about having said it. I still do at times.

Especially today, when we live in such an interconnected world and it's easy for someone to send an email or text asking for something, we can quickly become overloaded. I found that if

I wanted to succeed in my career while caring for my family and myself, it simply wasn't possible to spend a large chunk of time during the week saying yes to others' needs. We have all heard the saying *when you say yes to someone else, you are saying no to yourself.*

There are areas of life other than my career in which I'm compelled and open to saying "yes," such as when help is needed at my boys' school. I also don't want to be left out of fun with friends or my family. But I've found that if I say "yes" to too many activities, I'm in effect saying "no" to my own priorities.

It isn't easy to *just say "no."* Our ability to do so when it's needed depends on our fierce clarity about what really matters to us. Where is our energy best invested? I love to-do lists so my tasks stay on paper and out of my head where they will likely spin uncontrollably. In the last few years I started highlighting my top three to-do list items. These highlighted items are the things that will best serve my work and purpose in the world. Simply reflecting on what these items will be each day or week helps me focus on what really matters. My favorite resource on how to stay in flow and get more done by doing less is my friend Christine Carter's book, titled *"The Sweet Spot, How to Find Your Groove at Home and Work"*. She even offers an online program I have gone through called "The Science of Flow". This is a great resource for parents and creative workers alike! If you work at home the way

I do, it takes a special kind of mindset and dedication to stay focused.

STATING MY PURPOSE

When I left Twitter, I really wanted to focus my time in a purposeful way. One of my teachers, Wendy Palmer, suggested that I create a statement to live by that would guide me towards my purpose. She encouraged me to take my time in writing this. The first draft of my statement of purpose wasn't at all what I ended up with. I kept speaking it aloud—at home, in my car—allowing it to evolve, tinkering with it until it felt right. Here is what I ultimately came up with: "I am committed to raising consciousness in myself and the world, through my practice, my community, and my work." I remember the first time I said those words out loud and how true they felt.

A statement of purpose can become a North Star to help guide us in the many choices we are faced with every day. I consult mine before saying "yes" to anything, asking myself, does my involvement in the activity I'm being invited to participate in honor my statement of purpose? If it doesn't, I say "no."

Not just in our work, but as parents, it's vital we each come up with our own statement of intention. What deserves our time? It isn't possible to do everything, so we have to make choices. Do our choices honor the kind of work we seek to do in the world, the kind of parent we want to be, the kind of friend we will become?

In order to best integrate this statement into my life I created a screensaver for my computer, attached it to my bathroom mirror, and put up sticky notes all around so I made sure I bumped into it regularly. Using it as a guidepost really helped launch me into a new phase of my life with guiding intention.

What's Calling to You?

Being able to hear what's calling to us—which books to read, which teacher to study with, which practice to delve into—takes awareness. Without a quiet mind, we can't hear what's trying to come through. But if we pay attention, things have the opportunity to unfold at just the right moment.

To share how much the right timing matters, I was introduced to Byron Katie's work a long time before I was ready to begin working with it. At that time, a friend tried to do Katie's unique inquiry process with me, but I had no context for it. So I concluded, "It's not for me." and didn't think about it again.

Three years later I found myself sitting in my kitchen with my dear friend Megan Cowan, founder of the Mindful Schools. We were talking about different spiritual teachers and what they offered, and she mentioned how much she respected both Byron Katie and Eckhart Tolle. Considering I was already hooked on Eckhart's work, my interest was piqued, so we had a deeper conversation that day and I set out to explore Katie's work. I bought *Loving What Is*, ordered some of her CDs for my car, and began devouring her method. In Katie's words, "I discovered that when I believed my stressful thoughts, I suffered, but that when I didn't believe them, I didn't suffer, and that is true for every human being. Freedom is as simple as that. I found that suffering is optional. I found a joy within me that has never disappeared, not for a single moment. That joy is in everyone, always."

The more I used her inquiry process, the more I was able to

find humor in my stressful thoughts. When I believe my stressful thoughts, I suffer; whereas when I don't believe them, I don't suffer. It's as if the unconscious stream of thoughts in my mind had been driving the ship. I certainly don't mean to suggest that I began sitting around in bliss being in the moment all the time. However, I did increasingly experience more moments of presence and was able to connect with reality a whole lot more. I noticed how often I tuned into the stressful stories in my head and stopped catastrophizing situations so much. From this place of knowing I was able to take action with integrity much more of the time.

Of course, I already knew so much of these lessons from my mindfulness studies and practice, and by now my thoughts certainly had less of a hold on me. Katie's work accelerated my progress. In other words, I came to her work at just the right moment *for me*. Not a day sooner.

WELCOMING IT ALL

I've learned that whenever I have a thought that triggers stress, this thought needs to be questioned. And by questioned, I mean turned upside down and inside out. By doing this repeatedly, I've increasingly learned to be not only at peace but actually happy in the circumstance I'm in right now. Waiting to be happy, which so many of us do—when our kids leave for school, when we get in the car, when our husband buys us the ring, when we get the job—just isn't helpful. What if we could be here and be happy now?

This doesn't mean we don't have goals and strive for them. It means that all we actually have is each moment, moment by moment, so we need to be willing to welcome every single one of them, even if a particular moment feels miserable. And plenty of moments in our lives will feel miserable.

It may sound strange when I say that stressful moments can be a plus, not a negative. It's a plus because they are pointing us to the work we have yet to do—work that will lead to our freedom.

So while we want to say no in our lives to things that do not serve us, we don't want to make the mistake of saying no merely because we are unable to hold the discomfort of a particular moment. As we age and mature, one of the greatest gifts we receive is the possibility of holding the moments of our lives with more equanimity. We can tolerate more pain and uncertainty, and in doing so open ourselves up to more joy.

> As we age and mature, one of the greatest gifts we receive is the possibility of holding the moments of our lives with more equanimity. We can tolerate more pain and uncertainty, and in doing so open ourselves us up to more joy.

CHAPTER 20

MY MESSY SPIRITUALITY

"Perhaps ultimately, spiritual simply means experiencing wholeness and interconnectedness directly, a seeing that individuality and the totality are interwoven: that nothing is separate or extraneous. If you see in this way, then everything becomes spiritual in its deepest sense. Doing science is spiritual. So is washing the dishes."

– Jon Kabat- Zinn

WHEN I WAS LIVING in San Francisco in my mid-twenties before getting married and having a family, a friend said to me one day, "You have got to come to Glide Memorial Church." It was a Methodist church.

My response was basically, "Thanks, but no thanks!"

After some sweet and enthusiastic prodding, I eventually went. This was one of those times when allowing someone else to influence me turned out to be a super smart thing to do. The part of me that resisted was the aspect of me simply reacting to the religion of my early years.

I found myself with more than a thousand-people standing, singing, and celebrating on a rainy Sunday morning. With a ninety-person choir, and a band in full swing, the message at Glide was about total acceptance of everyone regardless of race, gender, or religion. In that moment, feeling so at home, tears just poured from my eyes. From then on, I attended often and felt even more settled in my new city of San Francisco. I enjoyed it so much that I became a regular volunteer, working with individuals who were getting off the streets and looking for jobs. Glide was a reassuring experience for me in that it was confirmation I was on the right track, in the right city, living a life that felt authentic and aligned to who I was.

If you live in San Francisco or are ever in the area, don't miss an opportunity to attend a Sunday "celebration" at Glide. They also offer opportunities to volunteer serving breakfast, lunch, and dinner to the at-risk community they serve. To this day I volunteer there, but now I bring my entire family. May we all have the opportunity to expose our children to communities who accept human beings just as they are.

Looking back, I appreciate every moment of pain and messiness that guided me along the way. I'm not even sure how to define my spiritual path other than to say it has emerged slowly and continues to keep me on my toes (kinda like parenting). The curveballs life throws feel less personal and more curious than they ever have. I can hold the "happy" and the "sad" at the same time in a way I just couldn't earlier in my life. Every day I learn to be kinder to myself.

Coming Home

Although I can't claim to subscribe wholeheartedly to any one spiritual tradition, I appreciate so many. For me, the only thing that has ever made sense is that all religions are the same story being told in a myriad of ways. We all belong to each other regardless of what house of worship we spend our time. I find a clear truth in the idea that we are all interconnected.

In discovering my path, I didn't "get" that the good, the bad, and the ugly was all there for my awakening. At first I saw spiritual practice in terms of my times of meditation, and whatever other forms of practice I had put in place for myself. It never occurred to me that raising a family can be a contemplative practice in and of itself. It became clear over time that the messier my days were, the more opportunity existed for me to see clearly, if only I was willing to put in the work to do so. And yes, it's OK to surrender into the mess and try again tomorrow. Sometimes you just have to take a bath and browse Netflix. Hall passes are critical.

After many years of practice, day long events, early morning meditations, online classes, reading books, coaching others, and being coached myself, I finally realized that coming home to my family is where I actually do my best learning and growing. Anyone who knows me will tell you that I'm pretty obsessed with discovering more about myself and how this whole being human thing works. As obsessed as I am with my studies and practices, nothing compares to a moment of stillness. Or silliness with my kiddos! Of really being here now.

In my 20's and early 30's, I hopped on and off my spiritual path, only slightly recognizing the signs that were gently nudging me to awaken just where I was. So it was, that my journey finally began at the ripe age of thirty-six, when one son went off to preschool and the other was barely out of my womb. This was over a decade after my interest in spirituality was first sparked. Life takes whatever time it needs to do its job thoroughly. Practicing mindfulness, meditation, and inquiry, in a myriad of ways would be where I would find my ultimate path.

I will always honor and love regular meditation practice and retreat, but also value just as much my practices, which are cleverly snuck in between preparing meals, driving kids around, developing my career, and participating in my day-to-day life.

Over time I increasingly find mindfulness practices "doing me," rather than me "doing them." It's just become part of who I am, and with practice this can be true for all of us. What parent doesn't want to live a life seeped more in "being" rather than so much "doing"? I don't know about you, but I'm exhausted from so much doing. Can we all just take a collective breath together?

Like most people when they think of having children, I pictured myself having the perfect "happy family." Before our kids actually arrive on the scene, don't most of us have all kinds of pink cloud ideas of what motherhood, being a father, and sitting around the dinner table, sharing stories from the day will be like?

Raising kids has stressed me, provoked me, angered me, and frazzled me unlike almost anything else in life—especially when I was trying to do it all on top of pursuing a career or simply making ends meet.

This is where awareness proves most valuable—it doesn't *require* going to a place of worship, setting up an altar, going off on retreats, or gathering with others to discuss lofty thoughts (although it's probably clear by now I'm a fan of all of those things). Though each of these can serve as tools on the journey to greater awareness, when and how we practice mindful awareness is ultimately up to us.

> Over time I increasingly find mindfulness practices "doing me," rather than me "doing them." It's just become part of who I am, and with practice this can be true for all of us

As we teach ourselves to live in this moment we automatically model this for our children. It won't be easy with the world and technology demanding our attention at every turn. As we regulate ourselves, they learn to do the same. When we talk through our struggles out loud, we give them permission to struggles themselves. As we openly admire the bright color and sweetness of summer blueberries so too will they notice such simple things. When we begin to see the ordinariness of life as extraordinary, we know we are on to something.

For so many years I looked for a place to belong, a place to call my own. And although I found those things in a new city and family life, nothing has compared to coming home to myself. Breath by breath, moment by moment. I was the one I was waiting for all along. Welcome home. Messiness and all.

ACKNOWLEDGEMENTS

Writing a book turns out to be fairly all encompassing, not unlike raising children. I owe many people thanks for helping me birth this book.

Special thanks to my editor David Ord. You are a brilliant writer and wonderful friend.

To my husband Riccardo, you are an amazing partner in this life. I feel so lucky to share this crazy ride of parenting with you.

Soren Gordhamer, my soul brother and dearest friend. Your guidance and love have always shined on my path, helping me to know which way to go.

Miss Pam Boney, my cosmic sister. You believe in me and always show up when I need you.

Leah Pearlman of Dharma Comics, who so generously provided the stick figure meditator on the cover of this book. Your creativity, generosity, and wisdom just blows me away. And to Michele Lilyanna who created the rest of the illustrations...you are generous beyond words.

To my friend Megan Cowan, who I can always trust to walk with me towards truth and never let me take myself too seriously.

A deep bow to all of my teachers (mentioned below and not mentioned) who I have studied and practiced with over the years: Byron Katie, Jon Kabat-Zinn, Will Kabat-Zinn, Dr. Shefali Tsabary, Jack Kornfield, Tara Brach, Dr. Dan Siegel, Wendy Palmer, and the faculty at Meridian University where I completed my Master's Degree.

Annmarie Chereso, Amy Rice-Jones, and Vanessa Donaldson.

You all met me in sisterhood to read these pages and offer me your feedback, editing expertise, and creativity. Thank you.

Huge amounts of gratitude go out to Jim Gimian, with whom I share a magical friendship. You were the first person to lay your eyes on this book and whisper into my ear that something special lay within its pages. Your belief in me and the support you have so generously offered made all the difference.

About the Illustrators

Michele Lilyanna is responsible for all of the beautiful images that pop up throughout this book. She taught in the Canadian public education system for over thirty years. Her teaching focused on social and emotional learning and artistic expression. She is the co-author, with James Baraz of Awakening Joy For Kids, awarded the 2016 Nautilus Gold medal. When Michele is not teaching parents, educators, or children, she is awakening joy on the Sunshine Coast of British Columbia with her partner, Peter, and her two sons.

Leah Pearlman is responsible for the sweet meditator on the cover of this book. She is the creator and founder of Dharma Comics, a popular web comic series. She is also the author of Drawn Together: Uplifting Comics on the curious Journey through Life and Love. She had originally started her career as a technologist, most recently working for Facebook where she co-created both Facebook pages and the Like button, the very features that later helped her comics spread.

CPSIA information can be obtained
at www.ICGtesting.com
Printed in the USA
LVHW02s1139261117
557608LV00003B/12/P